1920s Fashions

from
B. Altman & Company

DOVER PUBLICATIONS, INC.
Mineola, New York

Copyright

Copyright © 1999 by Dover Publications, Inc.
All rights reserved under Pan American and International Copyright Conventions.

Bibliographical Note

1920s Fashions from B. Altman & Company is a new work, first published by Dover
Publications, Inc., in 1999.

Library of Congress Cataloging-in-Publication Data

B. Altman & Co.
   1920s fashions from B. Altman & Company.
      p.   cm.
   ISBN 0-486-40293-2 (pbk.)
    1. Costume—United States—History—20th century. 2. Fashion—United States—
History—20th century. 3. B. Altman & Co. I. Title.
GT615.B2   1999
391'.009'0402—dc21   98-46318
                                                    CIP

Manufactured in the United States of America
Dover Publications, Inc., 31 East 2nd Street, Mineola, N.Y. 11501

PUBLISHER'S NOTE

By the beginning of the 1920s, New York's B. Altman and Company, founded in 1864, occupied an entire city block from Fifth Avenue to Madison Avenue and from Thirty-fourth Street to Thirty-fifth Street. Carrying everything from art objects and Oriental rugs to fancy needlework, the store was noted for its elegance and style and prided itself on its combination of quality and affordability:

> The name of Altman has, from the earliest days of the business, been regarded as a synonym for integrity, excellence of quality and efficiency of service. . . . [in addition] the house makes a special feature of its moderate prices. . . . offer[ing] their goods at prices that are frequently far below the actual market values.

Chief among the goods offered were, of course, the latest fashions for women. This collection of pages taken from Altman's seasonal catalogs chronicles the change from the post World War I fashions, with hems hovering just above the ankle, to the knee-skimming "flapper" costumes of the mid- to late-20s.

In addition to day and evening wear for women, these pages also feature lingerie and accessories such as hats and shoes, as well as clothing for boys and girls.

WOMEN'S TAILORED SUITS

Sizes 34 to 44; size 46 may be specially ordered

69S5 Sports Suit of worsted jersey, a material which does not stretch. The coat is cut with short shoulders and well-fitted sleeves, the back having a series of small cluster tucks. This suit is in sable, that new shade of dark tan, or in lovely bluet heather **$17.75**

69S5A The Sports Suit described in No. 69S5, may be specially ordered in navy blue or black **$17.75**

69S6 Smartly-tailored Suit of navy blue tricotine, the seams of which are bound with braid. This suit is cut on extremely attractive lines and may be worn without the belt, giving the new straight effect; the skirt is pocketed and the coat is silk-lined and averages about 31½ inches in length—a fashionable and becoming length, with the long lines accentuated. Beneath the mousquetaire gloves, the sleeves are wrist-length **$42.50**

69S6A Same style as No. 69S6 may be specially ordered in black, lined with black or gray **$42.50**

69S6B The Suits described in Nos. 69S6 and 69S6A may be specially ordered in sizes 44½, 46½ or 48½, cut on extra long lines, with extra fullness in skirt and sleeves, suitable for full figures . **$50.00**

69S7 Sports Suit of bluet or sable color homespun, the silk-lined coat with inverted plaits at the back, and the skirt with pockets. This shade of sable is very effective, and suggests a dark tan **$29.00**

69S7
$29.00

69S5

69S6
$42.50

69S5
$17.75

69S6

69S7

TAILORED SUITS, FROCKS AND WRAPS FOR JUNIOR MISSES

61S1 Junior Misses' Sports Suit of all-wool jersey, in brown or blue heather mixture. The unlined and belted coat is cut on straight lines, with tuxedo collar, while a smart inverted plait adorns the back and pockets; the skirt is slightly gathered under a belt and is pocketed; sizes 15 and 17 years $17.75

61S1
$17.75

61S3
$29.50

61S4
$25.00

61S2
$37.50

61S1

61S2

61S5

61S5
$6.75

61S6
$26.50

61S3

61S4

61S6

61S2 Junior Misses' Tailored Suit of navy blue serge. The box-coat, sketched with belt, may also be worn unbelted, has a fashionable collar and satin tie of youthful lines and is lined with silk pongee; the skirt is gathered under a belt and is finished with pockets; sizes 15 and 17 years $37.50
61S3 Junior Misses' Wrap-coat of Pekin blue or tan wool velour, lined throughout with silk. Rows of silk stitchings adorn the collar, the back of the wrap and the cuffs; the graceful sweep of the garment is held in by a belt in front; sizes 15 and 17 years .$29.50
61S4 Junior Misses' Afternoon Dress of crepe de chine, the soft lines being accentuated by the "trellis" design, revealing a contrasting shade, which also forms the modish collar and cuffs; draped girdle of self-material ties at the side; navy blue, with the contrasting color in henna; also in brown with tan; sizes 15 and 17 years $25.00
61S5 A very girlish Frock of checked gingham is shown in the sketch; a straight model with collar and cuffs of white pique prettily embroidered in contrasting shade of worsted; row of crocheted buttons adorns the waist, and the narrow belt ties at the side; large pockets; in a combination of colors, rose, blue or green predominating; sizes 15 and 17 years $6.75
61S6 Junior Misses' Afternoon Frock of navy blue silk taffeta, designed with corded tunic; the square neckline is accentuated by a collar of eyelet batiste; 15 and 17 years .$26.50

WOMEN'S FROCKS

Sizes 34 to 44; size 46 may be specially ordered

70S16 Developed in **navy blue Georgette crepe is this plaited frock,** which has quite a distinctive embellishment in the jet fringe which appears on the lower edge of the tunic skirt and on the sash. The collar of lace and the sleeves are of a charming mode   **$32.50**

70S16
$32.50

70S18
$49.50

70S16

70S17
$48.00

70S18

70S17 Afternoon Dress of light gray crepe de chine, made with flowing button-trimmed panels at the side. The collar is of hand-embroidered batiste **$48.00**
70S17A The gown described in No. 70S17 may be specially ordered with an elastic waistline, making it suitable for maternity wear, as it is a particularly graceful style **$52.50**
70S18 Of black satin which, as a material, lends itself to modes of great distinction, is this Gown fashioned on extremely smart lines. The embroidery is in black with a touch of gray **$49.50**

70S17

67S22
$9.75

63S21
$9.75

61S19
$9.75

62S20
$5.00

57S18
$8.25

WOMEN'S, MISSES' AND CHILDREN'S RAINCOATS, CAPES AND HATS

57S18 Girl's Raincoat and Hat of tan or navy blue rubberized cantonette. The coat is an attractive little model, with pockets, belt and modish collar and cuffs. The sleeves are in the raglan style; sizes 6 to 16 years **$8.25**

61S19 Junior Misses' Raincoat of navy blue or tan cantonette, of unusually good quality; raglan sleeves; smart convertible collar; attractive cuffs and pockets; sizes 15 and 17 years **$9.75**

62S20 Children's Raincape of navy blue or tan rubberized cantonette; hood with lining of plaid silk, sizes 2 to 5 years **$5.00**

63S21 Misses' Raincoat of tan rubberized cantonette, with a smart tailored belt, convertible collar, patch pockets, raglan sleeves and turn-back cuffs; sizes 14, 16, 18 and 20 years **$9.75**

67S22 Women's Raincoat of tan rubberized cantonette, with raglan sleeves, strap at wrist, belt, slashed pockets, and convertible collar. The yoke is lined with white mercerized material; length 52 inches; sizes 34 to 44 inches, bust measurement . . . **$9.75**

MISSES' OUTER COATS

Misses' sizes range as follows: 14 years, 32 inches, bust; 16 years, 34 inches, bust; 18 years, 36 inches, bust; 20 years, 38 inches, bust

63S1   Wrap developed in veldyne—an all-wool material, with a soft lustrous finish, featuring the new mandarin sleeve effect and patch pockets, the collar forming a throw, finished with heavy silk tassel; silk-lined throughout; in Sorrento blue or ostrich gray **$58.00**

63S2   Cape-wrap fashioned of marvella—one of the finest Bolivia fabrics made; with "Buster Brown" collar and tie; full flare sleeve effect; lined throughout with silk; in ostrich gray or Sorrento blue **$68.00**

63S2A   Same style as No. 63S2 of navy blue serge, lined throughout with silk **$29.50**

63S3   This Garment, fashioned of a homespun material, is modeled with a notch collar, plain tailored raglan sleeves, a two-inch plait in the center back, patch pockets and narrow belt; the yoke and sleeves are silk-lined; in blue-and-gray mixture, or in gray **$25.00**

63S4   This Cape is developed in marvella—one of the finest Bolivia fabrics made, and is designed on straight lines at the back. At either side there is a yoke effect from which the fullness falls, the collar showing a long shawl effect fastened with one button; silk-lined throughout; in Hindustan (light brown) or navy blue **$78.00**

52S7
$12.75

52S8
$9.85

52S9
$7.50

52S10
$7.90

52S11
$5.50

WOMEN'S AND MISSES' SWEATERS
A DIVERSITY OF STYLES

52S7   Women's and Misses' Sports Sweater of heavy-weight wool; with belt and pockets; in maroon or Copenhagen blue; sizes 36 to 44 inches, bust measurement **$12.75**

52S8   Women's and Misses' fiber Sweater, in an extremely smart weave, introducing a striped effect; tuxedo collar, cuffs, pockets and fringe-finished sash; in black, gray, tan or pink; sizes 34 to 44 inches, bust measurement . . . **$9.85**

52S9   Women's and Misses' worsted Sweater, in the plain stitch, with long revers and narrow sash. On the revers and cuffs a contrasting color is introduced in a striped effect—extremely smart, as the sweater is in tan with the contrasting touch in brown; also in black with the contrasting touch in white; sizes 36 to 44 inches, bust measurement **$7.50**

Should other styles than those illustrated be desired, additional information will be given on request.

52S10   Women's and Misses' Sweater of light-weight wool, with new roll collar, extending to the waistline; narrow sash; pockets; in champagne, orchid or Copenhagen; sizes 34 to 42 inches, bust measurement **$7.90**

52S11   Women's and Misses' light-weight worsted Sweater, a surpliced style, with tuxedo effect. The sweater is in a novelty weave, but the collar is in the plain stitch, as is the fringe-finished sash; in tan, navy blue or black; sizes 34 to 42 inches, bust measurement **$5.50**

34S4
$6.50

34S5
$4.00

34S6
$11.50

34S7
$3.50

34S13
$8.75

34S8
$12.00

34S9
$9.75

34S10
$16.10

34S11
$12.75

34S12
$3.50

34S14
$13.75

To facilitate the prompt and correct filling of Orders, it is suggested that the Order Blank (page 121) be used in every instance possible. Additional Order Blanks will be sent on request

MILLINERY

34S4 Mushroom shape of black transparent braid, with black satin bow **$6.50**
34S5 Sailor Hat of rough straw; a straight brim, trimmed with Georgette crepe which slips through the brim and hangs in a graceful streamer effect; in navy blue, with the crepe in two tones, navy blue and sand color; also in all-henna **$4.00**
34S6 Hat of black transparent braid combined with black straw; a smartly rolled brim, trimmed with black imitation paradise **$11.50**
34S7 Hat of hemp straw, with rolled brim, trimmed with Georgette crepe; in all-navy blue; also in henna with the Georgette crepe in navy blue **$3.50**
34S8 Mushroom shape of Copenhagen blue straw braid, with facing of sand-color straw; trimmed with wreath of colored flowers. **$12.00**
34S9 Sports Hat of stitched silk, with silk flower; in apple green or burnt orange **$9.75**

34S10 Turban of lisere straw, with ostrich forming the crown and curving gracefully at the right side; in all-black or all-henna, $16.00. *U. S. tax 10c., total* **$16.10**
34S11 Hat of hemp straw, with crown of faille silk and ends of self-material at the side back; in gray or pheasant brown . **$12.75**
34S12 Rolled-brim Sailor Hat of basket straw, with edge of hemp; in black or navy blue **$3.50**
34S13 Matron's Hat of black silk straw; with jet ornaments across the front **$8.75**
34S14 Matron's Hat of straw, trimmed with ostrich and spangled pin; the brim is of taffeta silk; in all-black, also in navy blue **$13.75**

BATHING SUITS, BEACH CAPES, CAPS AND SHOES

72S50 Women's Bathing Suit of black silk taffeta, made with the extremely fashionable ruffled skirt; tie sash of self-material; sizes 36, 38, 42, 44 inches, bust measurement **$18.50**

72S51 Bandana of rubberized satin; in navy blue, green, purple or red **$2.10**

72S52 Women's Bathing Suit of black or navy blue silk taffeta, trimmed with white soutache braid; wide girdle of self-material; sizes 36, 38, 42, 44 inches, bust measurement . . **$16.50**

72S53 Bathing Hat of rubberized black satin; Copenhagen, green or purple, a contrasting color in the upturned brim . . **$3.25**

72S54 Slippers of black canvas, with one button; sizes 3, 4, 5, 6 and 7; per pair . . . . **$ .75**

72S55 Women's One-piece Swimming Suit of black or navy blue wool jersey, emb. with contrasting color wool; tie sash of self-material, with a large tassel of wool; 36, 38, 42 and 44 in. bust **$9.85**

72S56 Diving Cap, heavy gray rubber, with chin-strap **$ .65**

72S57 Women's Bathing Suit of black silk poplin, trimmed with plaitings of self-material, and finished with buttons and tie sash; sizes 36, 38, 42 and 44 inches, bust measurement **$9.90**

72S58 Bathing Cap of rubber; assortment of colors **$ .55**

72S59 High Bathing Shoes of black satin; leather-trimmed; sizes 3, 4, 5, 6, 7; per pair **$3.50**

72S60 Beach Cape, Turkish toweling; rose or Copen.**$8.90**

72S61 Women's Bathing Suit of black surf satin, smartly piped with Copen., green or purple; closing on both shoulders; finished with buttons and tie sash; sizes 36, 38, 42 and 44 inches, bust **$6.90**

72S62 Diving Cap of heavy gray rubber . . . . **$ .50**

72S63 Misses' Bathing Suit, black silk poplin, emb. with contrasting color wool; finished with pockets; tie sash; 12, 14 and 16 yrs.**$8.75**

72S64 Children's one-piece Bathing Suit of wool jersey; in Copenhagen, navy blue or heather mixture; contrasting jersey on the collar, and forming the sash and bands; sizes 4, 6, and 8 . **$5.90**

72S65 Bathing Cap of rubber; in an assortment of colors **$ .35**

72S66 Slippers of black satin, ribbon lacings; sizes 3, 4, 5, 6 and 7; per pair . **$2.10**

54S189

14S184

88S205

28S186

28S185

RIDING ATTIRE

The Riding Habits, Separate Skirts and Breeches quoted are all custom-made in B. Altman & Co.'s own workrooms. B. Altman & Co., are prepared to meet all exacting requirements of the devotees of horseback riding. The illustrations are smart in the extreme and conform in every detail to the standards sanctioned by modern schools of riding. Women's Riding Habits are furnished in sizes 34 to 40 inches (bust); Misses' sizes, 14 to 18 years; and Children's sizes, 8 to 14 years. Women's sizes, 42 and 44 inches (bust) may be specially ordered, a few days being required to fill order. Women's and Misses' Separate Riding Breeches and Separate Divided Skirts, also Knickers, are in waistband measurements 26, 28, 30 and 32 in. In the Cloth Habits, Coats are lined with satin, and rubber-faced; Breeches are reinforced with chamois. In other materials, Coats are unlined, and Breeches reinforced with self-material.

14S184 Windsor Tie of satin; in black, navy blue, red or brown
        $ .50
28S185 Riding Crop of braided gray leather . . . $3.25
28S186 Riding Crop of twisted thread, stag-horn handle, sterling silver band, $2.50. U. S. tax, 13c., total . . . $2.63
53S187 Puttee Leggings of brown or black calfskin; 11 to 16 in., calf measurement (no half sizes); pair, $12.00. U. S. tax 20c., total $12.20
53S188 Women's Riding Boots of black or dark tan calfskin; sizes 2½, 3 and 3½, in B, C and D widths; 4 to 7½, in A to D widths; per pair, $25.00. U. S. tax $1.50, total $26.50
54S189 Riding Shirt of pongee silk, in the natural color; convertible collar; sizes 34 to 46 inches, bust measurement . . $6.75
54S189A Same style as No. 54S189, in all-white striped cotton madras $3.95

54S189B Same style as No. 54S189, in heavy-quality white Habutai silk $8.75
69S190 Women's and Misses' Riding Habit of tan linen (coat and breeches). The unlined coat has two pockets and the breeches are reinforced with self-material $21.00
69S190A Same style as No. 69S190; developed in cravenetted khaki $19.50
69S190B Similar model to No. 69S190 may be specially ordered in Oxford Melton; also in black-and-white checked worsted. $52.00
69S196 Children's Riding Habit (coat and breeches) of tan linen $19.50
69S196A Same style as No. 69S196 of cravenetted khaki (coat and breeches) $17.50
69S197 Women's and Misses' Breeches of cravenetted khaki; reinforced with self-material (not illustrated) . . . $7.75
69S198 Children's Riding Habit of tweed, with yoke effect; sizes 8 to 14 years, may be specially ordered . . . $38.00
69S199 Women's and Misses' Divided Skirt of cravenetted khaki may be specially ordered $8.75
69S200 Women's and Misses' Sports Knickers of cravenetted khaki may be specially ordered $7.75
88S205 Four-in-hand Scarf of silk, in attractive stripings $1.00

69S190

69S196

53S187

53S188

CHILDREN'S FROCKS AND HATS

38S30 Hat of charming design, fashioned of white or pink organdie; accordion-plaited brim and tucked crown; ribbon of black velvet; small flower of organdie **$6.75**

57S31 One-piece Frock of all-white dotted Swiss, or collar, cuffs, smocking and embroidery in Copenhagen blue; ties at back with bow-sash; sizes 6 to 10 years **$5.50**

57S32 Dress of pink or light blue organdie, with collar and cuffs in contrasting color; yoke and front of dress trimmed with worsted stitching and pompons; deep hem; 6 to 10 years **$4.90**

57S33 Dress of white lawn, with white smocking and embroidery—an unusually pretty style; sizes 6 to 10 years **$7.85**

57S34 One-piece Frock of white cotton voile, with narrow plaits at the center back and front, extending from the yoke. The collar, cuffs, flaps and deep band are of blue or maize cotton material, and the embroidery is in colors to match; sizes 6 to 10 years **$6.75**

57S35 Dress of light blue or maize organdie; skirt made with deep hem, scalloped and piped with white organdie; collar and cuffs finished with white piping. The dress is adorned with contrasting color hand-embroidered flowers; sizes 12 to 16 years **$7.25**

57S36 Dress of white cotton voile, trimmed with lace and ruffles, a girlish mode of great charm; sizes 8 to 14 years **$9.75**

57S31

57S32

38S30 $6.75

57S33

57S34

57S35

57S36

CHILDREN'S HATS AND OUTER COATS; ALSO SEPARATE SKIRTS

38S19 Hat of navy blue straw combined with self-color satin; rolled brim, and trimmed with cherries and narrow ribbon . . **$8.75**

38S20 Mushroom-shape of navy blue hemp straw, with edge of cerise straw, and colored motifs of velvet, stitched with worsted; **$5.50**

38S21 Hat of navy blue silk combined in self-color straw; a rolled brim, trimmed with pheasant-color silk and streamer . . **$8.00**

38S22 Tam o' Shanter of straw, black-and-blue combined; with colored pin . . . **$3.50**

38S23 Hat of Yeddo straw, rolled brim, and trimmed with colored worsted flowers and velvet ribbon; in Copenhagen blue or Tuscan **$10.50**

57S24 Regulation Reefer of navy blue storm serge; double-breasted, sailor collar, patch pockets, emblem on sleeve, brass buttons; white braid; sizes 6 to 12 years . . . **$12.75**

57S25 This Coat-wrap for the younger girl is made of tan or Pekin blue wool velour, in a double-breasted effect. The sleeves are trimmed with stitching, and tassels depend from the points of the collar; lined throughout with sateen; sizes 6 to 10 years **$13.50**

57S26 Sports Coat of wool jersey, in blue or brown heather mixture; the patch pockets, collar and cuffs are stitched; narrow belt buttons in front and is finished at the side with small buckles; sizes 10 to 16 years **$16.75**

57S27 Coat of silver-tip Bolivia, in reindeer or Copenhagen blue; lined throughout with sateen. Stitching adds to its attractiveness, and the coat is particularly smart; sizes 10 to 14 years **$21.50**

38S19 $8.75

38S20 $5.50

57S24

57S25

38S21 $8.00

38S22 $3.50

38S23 $10.50

57S26

57S29

57S27

57S28

57S28 Double-breasted Coat of tan or Copenhagen blue or silver-tone polo cloth, lined throughout with sateen; extremely smart; sizes 10 to 16 years **$16.50**

57S29 Box-plaited Skirt of all-wool plaid; tan and blue predominating; sizes 10 to 16 years **$10.50**

FASSO CORSETS; ALSO CORSETS AND ACCESSORIES FROM AMERICAN DESIGNERS

The Fasso Corset is made exclusively for B. Altman & Co., and is, possibly, more widely known than any other model ever designed by a French corsetiere. A number of Fasso models, developed in different materials, makes it possible for individual requirements to be met adequately, and in none of these models is comfort sacrificed for symmetry, as the Fasso is constructed on such scientific lines that absolute comfort is combined with grace of contour. Other French models are also represented in the assortments, in addition to the corsets and brassieres of American design, and further information will be given on request.

45S5   Fasso Corset of white or pink broche; boned with real whalebone and lace-trimmed; it is designed for medium or stout figures, is very low at the bustline and under the arms, long at the back and over the hips, with the cutaway effect below the front steel, and holds the diaphragm firmly; an elastic lacing for the front and a silk lacing (ten yards) are supplied with the corset; sizes 23 to 32, $22.50. *U. S. tax $1.75,* total **$24.25**

45S6   Bust Supporter and Diaphragm Confiner of a strong quality of pink silk tricotine, combined with fancy satin-striped material, and giving a very flat appearance when worn with a very low-top corset; sizes 34 to 46 . . . **$5.00**

45S7   Corset of pink cotton broche, with fancy band of elastic at the top, which is cut very low; boneless hips; well boned at back; eyelets below front steel; two pairs of attached hose supporters; sizes 21 to 30 . . . . **$4.50**

45S8   Corset of white coutil, trimmed with satin ribbon and lace; extremely low at top of bust and under arms; high back; long all around bottom; elastic gore at side of front; hook and eye, also eyelets below front steel; suitable for medium and stout figures; three pairs of hose supporters; sizes 22 to 32, $7.25. *U. S. tax 23c.,* total **$7.48**

45S9   Laced-front Corset of pink coutil, the top being very low and made of a band of strong fancy elastic; long skirt; suitable for the average figure; three pairs of attached hose supporters; sizes 22 to 30, $5.50. *U. S. tax 5c.,* total **$5.55**

45S10   Corset of pink silk broche; designed especially for stout figures; well boned back and front; boneless hip; very low back and front, and extremely so under arms, with an elastic at waist to prevent binding; very long at bottom of back and hip; medium in front, with elastic gore and eyelets below front steel; three pairs of attached hose supporters; sizes 22 to 36, $14.25. *U. S. tax 93c.,* total **$15.18**

Special attention is given all correspondence; individual requirements are carefully considered, and corsets are selected by expert corsetieres.
In instances where the merchandise is subject to the U. S. tax, the price on the illustration includes the tax.

UNDERGARMENTS OF AMERICAN DESIGN; ALSO BOUDOIR CAPS

47S74 Nightrobe of nainsook; edge of Valenciennes lace; kimono sleeves; sizes 14 to 17 inches $1.50
47S75 Nightrobe of nainsook; empire effect; Valenciennes lace and tucking; sleeveless; sizes 14 to 16 inches . $3.50
47S76 Nightrobe of cambric, with tucked yoke and edge of embroidery; sizes 14 to 17 inches $2.35
47S76A Same style as No. 47S76; extra size, 18 inches $3.00
47S77 Nightrobe of nainsook; empire effect; insertion of embroidery; Valenciennes lace; kimono sleeves; 14 to 17 in. $1.95
47S78 Nightrobe of nainsook, elaborately trimmed with Valenciennes lace; short set-in sleeves; sizes 14 to 17 inches $3.75
47S79 Nightrobe of nainsook; kimono sleeves; empire effect, with insertion of narrow Valenciennes lace; sizes 14 to 16 inches $2.90
47S80 Combination (Corset Cover and Drawers) of nainsook; tucking; Valenciennes lace, beading and ribbon; sizes 36 to 44 inches, bust measurement . . $2.90
47S80A Same style as No. 47S80; Corset Cover and Petticoat . . . $3.50
47S81 Corset Cover of nainsook; medallions of embroidery; and Valenciennes lace; sizes 36 to 44 inches, bust measurement . . . $1.25
47S82 Envelope Chemise of Nainsook; insertion of embroidery with narrow edge of Valenciennes lace; shoulder straps of embroidery and lace; sizes 36 to 44 inches, bust measurement . . $3.00
47S83 Chemise of nainsook; a regulation model, with Valenciennes lace; sizes 36 to 44 inches, bust measurement (matches Step-in Drawers No. 47S84) . . . $2.50
47S84 Step-in Drawers of nainsook; insertion and edge of Valenciennes lace; lengths 23 and 25 inches (matches Chemise No. 47S83) $2.35
47S85 Petticoat of cambric, with underlay; ruffle with insertions of Valenciennes lace and edge; 32 inches, waist; lengths 34, 36 and 38 inches $2.75
47S86 Petticoat of cambric, with ruffle of embroidery (no underlay); 32 inches, waist; lengths 34, 36 and 38 inches $2.25
47S87 Drawers of nainsook, with insertion and edge of Valenciennes lace; lengths 23, 25 and 27 inches (open) $2.10
47S87A Same style as No. 47S87 (closed) $2.10
47S87B Same as above, in extra size (open only); lengths 23, 25 and 27 in. $2.45
47S88 Drawers of cambric, with ruffle of embroidery; cluster tucking above; lengths 23, 25 and 27 inches (open) . . . $1.95
47S88A Same style as No. 47S88; in extra size, lengths 23, 25 and 27 in. $2.25
47S88B Same style as above (closed) . . . $2.25
47S89 Envelope Chemise of nainsook; Valenciennes lace, forming empire effect; ribbon shoulder straps; sizes 36 to 44 inches, bust measurement . . . $2.25
55S90 Dainty Boudoir Cap of blue, pink or lavender silk, with wired-ear effect, trimmed with lace, and blue, pink or lavender ribbon $1.75

55S91 Dainty Bandeau of lace and ribbon, which ties at the back; blue, pink or lavender ribbon $2.25

JUVENILE STYLES

49S41 Boys' Suit of chambray, in a combination of colors, with hand-stitching in contrasting silks; in tan stitched with brown, or blue with the stitching in Copenhagen blue; the trousers, collar, cuffs and laps on pockets are of the darker shade; sizes 2 to 4 years **$3.35**

49S42 Boys' Suit; trousers of blue or brown Devonshire, with blouse of striped dimity; hand-stitching; sizes 2 to 5 years **$3.75**

49S43 Boys' Suit of brown or blue chambray, trimmed with white braid; sizes 2 to 4 years . **$2.95**

49S44 Boys' Suit; trousers of blue or green Devonshire, with blouse of white poplin; hand-embroidery; sizes 2 to 5 years **$3.40**

49S45 Boys' Suit; trousers of bisque or green chambray, with blouse of white striped dimity; hand-stitching; sizes 2 to 5 years **$3.90**

49S46 Boys' Suit; trousers of green or maize Devonshire; blouse of white striped madras; 2 to 5 yrs. **$3.00**

49S47 Boys' Suit; trousers of blue or tan chambray; blouse of white striped madras; sizes 2 to 5 years **$2.45**

49S47A Same style as No. 49S47 of tan chambray; cuffs of white poplin; collar edged with white poplin; sizes 2 to 5 years **$2.45**

49S48 Boys' Suit; trousers, collar and cuffs of blue Devonshire; blouse of white poplin; sizes 2 to 5 years **$3.45**

49S49 Dress of blue chambray, trimmed with white braid; red tie; 2 to 5 yrs. **$2.45**

49S50 Dress of blue or red checked gingham, collar cuffs, and laps on pockets are of white pique, with silk stitching to match check; sizes 2 to 5 years **$2.25**

49S51 Bloomer Dress of green or blue chambray, hand-stitching and hand-embroidery; sizes 2 to 5 years **$3.25**

49S52 Bloomer Dress of lavender or blue checked gingham, trimmed with white bindings and a silk hand-stitch in self-color; sizes 2 to 5 years . **$3.75**

49S53 Bloomer Dress of tan or blue chambray, trimmed with a darker shade of brown or blue; sizes 2 to 5 years; **$2.10**

49S54 Bloomer Dress of blue chambray, with rose stitching; 2 to 5 yrs. **$2.45**

49S55 Bloomer Dress of tan or green chambray, with hand-stitching; sizes 2 to 5 yrs. **$4.10**

49S56 Boys' Suit; trousers of maize or lavender chambray; blouse of white poplin; collar and cuffs trimmed with Devonshire, hand-embroidered; sizes 2 to 4 years **$3.45**

62S81 Hat of white dimity; lace-trimmed; sizes 2 to 4 years **$2.10**

62S82 Hat of white pique; sizes 1 to 2 years **$1.10**

62S83 Hand-made Cap of white muslin; tucks, feather-stitching and lace; infants' to 2 yrs. **$1.85**

62S84 Cap of white dotted Swiss; with turn-back frill; lace edge; sizes 6 months to 2 years **$3.00**

62S85 Hat of white pique; with button-on crown; sizes 1 to 3 years . . . . . **$ .85**

62S86 Hand-made Cap of white muslin; hand feather-stitched and tucked; infants' to 2 yrs **$1.35**

62S87 Hat of Copenhagen blue or pink organdie; sizes 3 to 5 years **$2.45**

62S88 Cap of white dotted Swiss; embroidery and lace; sizes infants' to 2 years . . **$1.75**

PLAYTHINGS FOR BABYHOOD, AND THE BABY'S FIRST SHOES

49S241 Cat of gray plush . . . **$1.55**

49S242 Celluloid Rattle; hand-painted ribbon . . **$. 50**

49S243 Rabbit of gray plush, with voice apparatus **$1.35**

49S244 Satin-covered Hanger; hand-painted bow; in blue or pink . . **$ .90**

49S245 Four-piece hand-painted Toilet Set of celluloid **$1.90**

49S246 Rattle of celluloid . **$ .75**

49S247 Two-piece hand-painted Toilet Set of celluloid **$ .95**

49S248 Farmer Boy of stockinet. **$1.25**
49S249 Farmer Girl of stockinet. **$1.25**

49S250 Floating Set of celluloid . . . . **$ .85**

49S251 Pig of terry cloth, with voice apparatus . . . . **$ .65**

49S252 Rubber Water Bag; hand-painted . **$ .95**

49S253 Wooden Clothes Hanger, with girl or boy faces **$ .50**

49S254 Clown Rattle; celluloid; hand-painted ribbon . **$ .75**
49S255 Hand-painted floating Bath Thermometer **$1.15**

49S256 Carriage Strap of blue or pink satin, with teething ring and toy **$1.65**

49S257 Clown of stockinet; combination of black and orange **$1.10**

49S258 Keep Warm Clips (to hold bed clothes in position) . . . **$1.50**

49S259 Beaded Doll . **$ .60**
49S260 Egg Roly Poly, with duck; celluloid . . . . **$ .55**
49S261 Duck of yellow plush **$ .85**

49S262 Celluloid Clamps; hand-painted **$ .55**

49S263 Rattle; celluloid; hand-painted decoration in chicken design **$1.35**
49S264 Soft-soled Ankle Ties of kidskin; in white, tan or black; per pair **$1.00**
49S265 Soft-soled Shoes of kidskin; in white, black or tan; sizes 1, 2 and 3 . . . . . . **$1.10**

49S266 Strap of tan leather . . . **$ .55**

49S267 Egg-shaped Rattle; celluloid; hand-painted bow **$1.15**

49S268 Rattle; celluloid (egg shaped) **$ .50**

49S269 Moccasins of white kidskin, trimmed with white, blue or pink ribbon; size 2; per pair **$1.10**

49S270 Teething Ring; celluloid . . . . **$ .30**
49S270A Ivory Teething Ring **$ .75**

49S271 Record Book; covered with pink or blue moiré silk, with hand-painted decorations and colored pictures; to keep a record of childhood yrs. **$1.85**

58S78 $2.75

58S79 $1.25

58S80 $2.00

58S81 $2.00

58S82 $2.75

58S83 $4.50

58S84 $2.00

58S85 $3.95

88S94 $1.95

88S95 $1.75

BOYS' FURNISHINGS
(Illustrated on opposite page)

88S27 Four-in-hand silk Scarf; in attractive colored stripings $1.00

88S28 Shirt, neckband style, of fine quality cotton shirting ; in a variety of attractive colored stripings ; sizes 12 to 14 neckband $1.95

88S29 Two-piece Pajamas of percale, in a variety of colored stripings ; sizes 4, 6, 8, 10, 12, 14, 16 and 18 years $1.65

88S30 Pajamas of fine white cotton material, in one-piece style; also tan (88S30A), or blue (88S30B); 4, 6, 8, 10, 12, 14 and 16 years $1.50

88S31 Sports Shirt of white Oxford, with attached collar in polo style ; sizes 12 to 14 neckband $2.25

88S32 Four-in-hand silk Scarf ; in attractive stripings $1.00

88S33 Blouse of an unusually fine quality cotton shirting ; in attractive stripings ; in neckband style; sizes 8 to 14 years $1.50

88S34 Four-in-hand silk Scarf ; attractive patterns $.75

88S35 Sports Blouse of white Oxford ; sizes 7 to 14 years $1.50

88S36 Sports Blouse of fine percale ; in a variety of attractive stripings ; sizes 7 to 14 years $1.25

88S37 Blouse of an unusually fine quality cotton shirting, in colored stripings ; with attached collar in polo style ; in sizes 8 to 14 years $1.50

88S38 Blouse of madras, with attached Eton collar ; in a variety of colored stripings ; sizes 4 to 10 years $1.25

88S39 Knee Trousers of navy blue serge, lined throughout; sizes 4 to 10 years $3.50

88S40 Sports blouse of cotton khaki, a strong fast-color material ; sizes 7 to 14 years $.95

88S41 Knickerbockers of strong twilled cotton khaki; washable; well made; thoroughly reinforced; sizes 8 to 17 years $1.50

88S42 Blouse of white Oxford, with attached Eton collar ; sizes 4 to 10 yrs. $1.50

88S43 Knee Trousers of cotton khaki or white galatea, good quality, fast color ; sizes 4 to 10 years $1.15

88S44 Middy Blouse of blue jean ; regulation style, with double yoke, and emblem ; also in khaki-color (88S44A); sizes 4, 6, 8 and 10 years $2.45

88S45 Sweater of light-weight navy blue brushed yarn ; a pull-over-head V-neck style ; also in tan (88S45A); sizes 26, 28, 30, 32 and 34 inches, chest . $5.75

88S46 Middy Blouse of white jean, with blue collar and cuffs ; regulation style with double yoke, and emblem ; sizes 4, 6, 8 and 10 years $2.45

88S47 Suspender-waist of white webbing ; sizes 4, 6, 8, 10, 12 and 14 years $.95

88S48 Knickerbockers of drab-color corduroy ; lined throughout; sizes 8 to 17 years $2.95

88S49 Belt of black leather ; also in tan (88S49A); sizes 26, 28, 30, 32 and 34 inches $.95

BOYS' HATS AND SPECIALTIES
(Illustrated on this page)

58S78 Hat of black straw, in rolling-brim style, with medium crown ; sizes 6⅜ to 7 $2.75

58S79 Tam o' Shanter of white galatea ; sizes 6⅜ to 7 $1.25

58S80 Hat of brown straw ; turn-down brim, with band of silk grosgrain ribbon; also in blue (58S80A); sizes 6⅜ to 6⅞ $2.00

58S81 "Jack Tar" Hat of navy blue straw, with rolling brim ; sizes 6⅜ to 6⅞ $2.00

58S82 Hat of white straw, rolling brim, with medium crown ; sizes 6⅜ to 7 $2.75

58S83 Hat of white straw, excellent quality ; sizes 6½ to 6⅞ $4.50

58S84 Hat of navy blue straw ; a small shape with turn-down brim ; sizes 6⅜ to 7 $2.00

58S85 Hat of brown straw, rolling brim ; silk ribbon band ; sizes 6⅜ to 6⅞ $3.95

58S88 Regulation Naval Hat of white drill ; sizes 6⅜ to 7 . $.50

58S89 Tam o' Shanter of blue serge ; lettered band; 6⅜ to 7 $1.95

58S90 Regulation Middy Suit of white galatea, with collar and cuffs of washable blue serge ; a well-tailored suit, built on smart lines ; sizes 4 to 10 years $5.75

58S91 Middy Suit of blue serge, of excellent grade (all-wool); regulation navy style, with yoke and emblem ; black silk tie ; sizes 4 to 10 years . $8.95

58S88 50¢

58S89 $1.95

88S93 $1.00

58S90 $5.75

58S92 $1.75

58S91 $8.95

58S92 Overall of blue cotton material, light weight, but strong quality; combines a blouse and overall in one piece; 4, 6, 8 and 10 yrs. $1.75

58S93 Overall of a blue cotton fabric, trimmed with red ; sizes 4, 6, 8 and 10 years . $1.00

88S94 Golf Cap of blue serge ; sizes 6⅝ to 7⅛ . $1.95

88S95 Golf Cap, of fine woolen material ; in brown ; also in gray (88S95A) ; sizes 6⅝ to 7⅛ . $1.75

58S116
$4.75

58S117
$4.75

58S118
$3.95

58S120
$4.25

58S119
$3.50

58S121
$2.95

58S122
$3.25

58S123
$3.25

58S124
$3.95

58S125
$2.95

BOYS' WASHABLE SUITS

(Guaranteed fast color)

58S116 In the French blouse style is this Suit of blue linen-finished suiting, with collar and cuffs of washable blue serge; emblem on sleeve; cord and whistle; 3 to 8 years. **$4.75**

58S117 Suit of white jean, with collar and cuffs of washable blue serge; in French blouse style; emblem on sleeve; 3 to 8 years. **$4.75**

58S118 Suit of white rep, in a sailor style model; collar and cuffs of cadet blue suiting, trimmed with white braid; emblem on sleeve; cord and whistle; sizes 3 to 8 years. **$3.95**

58S119 Middy Suit of khaki jean, well-tailored; a regulation model, with taping, yoke and emblem; black silk tie; 4 to 10 yrs. **$3.50**

58S120 Suit, in an English middy style, made of blue linen-finished suiting with white embroidery and taping; sizes 4 to 10 years **$4.25**

58S121 Suit, comprising blouse of white rep and trousers of blue chambray; trimming of white braid; collar and cuffs match the trousers; sizes 3 to 7 years **$2.95**

58S122 Sailor model, comprising blouse of tan cotton crash and trousers of blue chambray; trousers copied from sailor broadfall style; cord and whistle; sizes 3 to 8 years . **$3.25**

58S123 Middy Suit of tan cotton crash, a neat model trimmed with black braid and black silk tie; 4 to 10 years **$3.25**

58S124 Suit, in an English middy style; blouse made of woven-striped cotton suiting; trousers of plain-color cotton material, as are the collar and cuffs; in blue; also in brown (58S124A); emblem on sleeve; sizes 4 to 10 years **$3.95**

58S125 Middy Suit of brown mixed chambray, attractively trimmed with white banding; black silk tie; also in green (58S125A); sizes 4 to 10 years **$2.95**

WOMEN'S OUTER COATS, CAPES AND WRAPS

Sizes 34 to 44

The Department for Women's Wraps, Capes and Coats provides every opportunity for the selection of sumptuous garments, as well as for the practical coat, for sports, motoring or general wear. Correspondence is invited, and additional information will be sent on request.

67F30
$52.50

67F32
$98.00

67F33
$42.50

67F31
$78.00

67F30 This Cape of black veldyne has a collar of gray lapin fur (gray hare) and is lined throughout with gray crepe de Chine; length 49 inches . **$52.50**

67F32 Coat of brown gerona cloth (similar to marvella), with attractive collar of beaver, a belted model with slashed pockets; lined throughout with self-colored crepe de Chine; also in navy blue or black with squirrel collar and lining of gray crepe; length 49 inches . **$98.00**

67F31 Wrap of navy blue or brown arabella cloth, lined throughout with crepe de Chine, and fur collared. In the navy blue model the collar is of squirrel and the lining of gray crepe de Chine, and in the brown model the collar is of beaver and the lining of self-color crepe; length 49 inches **$78.00**

67F33 Coat of tweed in a tan-and-brown mixture, with shawl collar of raccoon; a belted model, with raglan sleeves, an inverted plait at the back and patch pockets. Silk-lined throughout; length 48 inches **$42.50**

WOMEN'S OUTER COATS AND WRAPS

Sizes 34 to 44

67F43 Wrap of navy blue rivolai cloth, fashioned on becoming lines, and lined throughout with self-color crepe de Chine; length 49 inches **$32.50**

67F44 Coat of brown bolivia; a belted model, with deep arm size and slashed pockets. The collar is convertible, and the lining is of brown crepe de Chine; length 49 inches **$38.00**

67F45 Coat of brown delysia cloth, with collar and cuffs of wolf. This is a belted model, with raglan sleeves and slashed pockets; the lining throughout of silk; length 49 inches **$58.00**

67F46 Of navy blue bolivia, this model hangs unconfined at the back, the wide sleeves falling in the kimono effect. At the back, there are three rows of silk stitching, and the collar and bands on the sleeves are of black karakul kid. The coat is lined throughout with self-color crepe de Chine; length 49 inches **$49.00**

To facilitate the prompt and correct filling of Orders, it is suggested that the Order Blank (page 97) be used in every instance possible. Additional Order Blanks will be sent on request

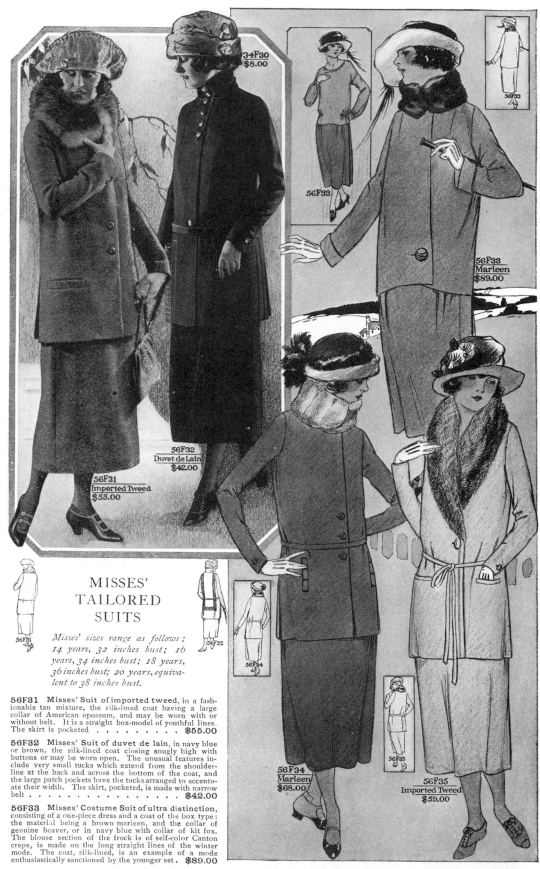

34F30
$8.00

56F33

56F33
Marleen
$89.00

56F31

56F32

56F32
Duvet de Lain
$42.00

56F31
Imported Tweed
$55.00

56F34

56F35

56F34
Marleen
$68.00

56F35
Imported Tweed
$59.00

MISSES' TAILORED SUITS

Misses' sizes range as follows: 14 years, 32 inches bust; 16 years, 34 inches bust; 18 years, 36 inches bust; 20 years, equivalent to 38 inches bust.

56F31 Misses' Suit of imported tweed, in a fashionable tan mixture, the silk-lined coat having a large collar of American opossum, and may be worn with or without belt. It is a straight box-model of youthful lines. The skirt is pocketed $55.00

56F32 Misses' Suit of duvet de lain, in navy blue or brown, the silk-lined coat closing snugly high with buttons or may be worn open. The unusual features include very small tucks which extend from the shoulderline at the back and across the bottom of the coat, and the large patch pockets have the tucks arranged to accentuate their width. The skirt, pocketed, is made with narrow belt $42.00

56F33 Misses' Costume Suit of ultra distinction, consisting of a one-piece dress and a coat of the box type: the material being a brown marleen, and the collar of genuine beaver, or in navy blue with collar of kit fox. The blouse section of the frock is of self-color Canton crepe, is made on the long straight lines of the winter mode. The coat, silk-lined, is an example of a mode enthusiastically sanctioned by the younger set. $89.00

56F34 Marleen, a charming material which the autumn has just introduced, is employed in this Misses' Suit, the coat of which is collared with squirrel, and has a narrow belt and slashed pockets. The regulation skirt is a two-piece model, with pockets and belt. The material is in navy blue or black, both models having a squirrel collar $68.00

56F35 Imported tweed in a tan mixture is employed in this Suit for the younger set, the silk-lined coat of which has a detachable shawl collar of natural raccoon, patch pockets and a narrow belt; regulation skirt is a two-piece model, with pockets and belt $59.00

34F30 This attractive duvetyn Hat is also illustrated on page 25, and a description in full will be found on that page.

MISSES' TAILORED SUITS

Misses' sizes range as follows: 14 years, 32 inches bust; 16 years, 34 inches bust; 18 years, 36 inches bust; 20 years, equivalent to 38 inches bust.

56F36 Imported tweed, a material adapted for sports wear or for general use, in a fashionable brown mixture, makes this Misses' Suit eminently practical, the collar being convertible, and the coat finished with pockets and a narrow belt. The skirt has a belt and pockets that correspond with those on the coat **$29.50**

56F37 Smartly tailored is this Misses' Suit of tweed in brown or tan mixture, the coat with its unusual pockets of the patch type, finished with a button-trimmed strap, the long roll, notched collar of unusual lines, the narrow belt and novelty bone buttons. The skirt with pockets and belt—a suit of many good points **$34.00**

56F38 Misses' Suit of duvet de lain, in navy blue or brown, with a particularly smart coat. Fine tucks are arranged in clusters the entire length of the coat at the back, outline the large pockets and also appear on the bell-shaped sleeves. The collar of wolf closes fashionably high or may be worn open. The regulation skirt is pocketed and made with belt **$57.00**

56F38A The Suit illustrated in No. 56F38 may be specially ordered in black **$57.00**

56F39 Misses' Suit of tweed, quite striking in the diagonal closing of the silk-lined coat, the self-color stitching, and the one pocket, which the camera does not record distinctly, being distinguishing features. Collared with fur—a luxurious effect is achieved. Tailored along straight lines is the pocketed skirt; in tan mixture with collar of natural raccoon or in gray mixture with collar of opossum . . . **$52.50**

NOTE—The Hats illustrated with the Suits and Frocks throughout the Catalogue are from B. Altman & Co.'s own ateliers. Accessories, including bags, umbrellas, walking sticks, etc., are from the various departments. The footwear may also be considered typical of the assortments for the current season.

34F32 $9.75

56F36 Imported Tweed $29.50

56F37 Tweed $34.00

56F40 Tweed $39.75

56F39 Tweed $52.50

56F38 Duvet de Lain $57.00

56F40 Misses' Three-piece Knicker Suit, comprising skirt, knickers and a silk-lined coat, the material a smart tweed, in black-and-white or tan. This is a decided sports model, the coat with plaited back and large patch pockets, a notched collar and a narrow belt; skirt, a regulation model, with patch pockets, and the knickers of the modern sports type; suitable for hiking, golfing or other sports occasions . **$39.75**

56F40A The Three-piece Suit illustrated in No. 56F40 is also obtainable in brown corduroy **$32.50**

34F32 The use of braid embroidery on the season's hats is seen on this model, a full description of which will be found on page 25, where another view of this hat is shown.

WOMEN'S AND MISSES' SEMI-MADE DRESSES AND SKIRTS

Sizes of Semi-made Skirts range as follows:

Waist	26	28	30	32	34	inches
Lengths	35	35	36	36	37	inches

Larger sizes can be specially ordered at additional cost for extra material

31F30
$9.75

31F30   78F53

78F53
$10.50

57F48
$10.85

57F49
$5.50

57F48

57F49

78F50
$9.50

78F54
$11.50

78F50

78F54

78F51
$10.75

78F52
$12.50

78F51

78F52

31F31
$17.50

NOTE—These Semi-made Dresses and Skirts require very little sewing to complete.

31F31 A most attractive model is this Semi-made Dress of silk-and-wool French crepe, which is in black embroidered in black, navy blue with black or self-color embroidery, or dark brown with self-color embroidery; sizes 36 to 44 inches bust. Special value at the extremely low price of **$17.50**

31F30 Semi-made Skirt of superior-quality all-wool checked worsted; in blue-and-tan, brown-and-tan or black-and-white (half-inch check; a smartly box-plaited model **$9.75**
31F30A Similar style to No. 31F30, with cluster plaits . **$9.75**

MISSES' READY-TO-WEAR SKIRTS

Sizes are mentioned in the descriptions

57F48 Misses' Plaited Skirt of fine-quality wool velour, in a fashionable check and in attractive colorings. The smart simplicity is enhanced by the perfect tailoring; in navy blue-and-tan, brown-and-tan or black-and-white; sizes 14, 16, 18 and 20 years **$10.85**
57F49 Misses' "Wrap-around" Skirt of an all-wool material, in a broad check; the pocket and side effect are attractively trimmed with rows of self-color stitching; novelty buttons; in brown-and-tan or navy blue-and-tan checks; sizes 14, 16, 18 and 20 years **$5.50**

WOMEN'S READY-TO-WEAR SKIRTS

NOTE—Women's Ready-to-wear Skirts are maintained in the following sizes (for larger sizes see No. 78F54):

Waist	26	28	30	32	34	inches
Lengths	34	35	35	36	36	inches

78F50 Women's Ready-to-wear Skirt of an all-wool checked material, suitable for sports wear; a tailored model, with slashed pockets; in blue-and-tan or brown-and-tan . . . **$9.50**

78F51 Women's Ready-to-wear Skirt of all-wool prunella cloth, with eponge stripes in contrasting color. A particularly attractive model, with double box-plaits; in black with white stripes, navy blue with tan stripes or brown with tan stripes **$10.75**

78F52 Women's Ready-to-wear Skirt of spiral crepe, made in combination box and side-plaits, with belt trimmed with buckle; in black or navy blue; the black is suitable for mourning wear **$12.50**

78F53 Women's Ready-to-wear Skirt of all-wool striped eponge, a sport model, smartly tailored, with slashed pockets and button-trimmed belt; in navy blue with tan and introducing narrow Persian stripes; in brown with tan and Persian stripes; also in black with white and Persian stripes; an extremely effective model **$10.50**

78F54 Women's Ready-to-wear Skirt, all-wool serge (in extra large sizes), smartly tailored, with panel front, gathered back, button-trim pocket and button-trim. belt; in black or navy blue; sizes as follows:

Waist	32	34	36	38	40	42	44	inches
Lengths	36	36	36	38	38	39	39	inches

$11.50

7F81
$3.95

7F82
Habutai
$8.75

7F83 Dimity $5.90
7F84 Broadcloth $11.75

7F85
Oxford
$4.95

7F86 Madras $5.50
7F87 Pongee $8.50

7F92
Wool Jersey
$7.90

7F89
Radium
$10.50

7F90 Crepe de Chine $9.75

7F91
$7.95

7F88
$2.95

TAILORED BLOUSES

The sizes are mentioned in the descriptions, and when Misses' sizes are not specifically given, sizes 34, 36 and 38 are equivalent to 16, 18 and 20 years

7F81 Small frills, together with real filet laces, make this a distinctive blouse, a white French voile being employed. Its graceful lines are made more pronounced by the long inserts of the lace; sizes 34 to 42 . . . . $3.95

7F82 The emphasis on this Blouse of white Habutai silk is in the smart new flat collar, which is most becoming to all types. The tucked bosom and the pearl buttons, and its superior tailoring all add a distinctive note; sizes 36 to 44 . . . . $8.75

7F82A The Model No. 7F82, may be specially ordered in extra sizes, 48 and 50 inches bust. (10 days being required) $10.50

7F83 The Blouse quoted in No. 7F82, is also obtainable in white imported striped dimity; sizes 36 to 44 . . . .$5.90

7F83A Same style as No. 7F83, may be specially ordered in extra sizes, 48 and 50 inches bust (10 days being required) $6.90

7F84 The Blouse illustrated in No. 7F82, is also obtainable in white broadcloth silk; sizes 36 to 44 . . . .$11.75

7F84A The Blouse, No. 7F84, may be specially ordered in extra sizes, 48 and 50 inches bust (10 days being required) $13.50

7F85 To meet the requirements for tennis, golf, riding and other uses, is this Sports Model of white basket weave material, known as Oxford cloth. The new features for this type of blouse are the collar, the inverted pocket, and the back which conforms to the lines of a man's golf coat, that open box-plaited effect, which provides freedom for the arms; sizes 34 to 46 . . . . . . $4.95

7F86 The Blouse illustrated in No.7F85, is also obtainable in white striped madras; sizes 34 to 46 . . . .$5.50

7F87 The Blouse illustrated in No.7F85, is also obtainable in tan pongee; 34 to 46 $8.50

7F88 For wear with sweaters or other purposes is this Blouse of white checked dimity. Very youthful is the collar, inserted with an interesting open design, as are the turn-back, linked cuffs. The narrow tucks contribute to its effectiveness; 34 to 42 $2.95

7F89 The tucked bosom is an attractive feature of this well-tailored Shirt of heavy-quality white radium silk, and the narrow plaiting which edges the collar and the linked, turn-back cuffs gives distinction; the buttons are of pearl; sizes 34 to 46 $10.50

7F90 The Shirt illustrated in No. 7F89, in heavy-quality white crepe de Chine; sizes 34 to 46 . . . .$9.75

7F91 Suitable for the mourning wardrobe is this Blouse of heavy-quality black crepe de Chine. The long roll collar, vestee and turn-back cuffs are adorned with small braided buttons. The hemstitching is an attractive note; sizes 36 to 44 . . . . . . $7.95

7F91A Same style as No. 7F91, may be specially ordered in extra sizes, 48 and 50 inches bust (10 days being required) $9.50

7F92 Wool Jersey, a fabric so universally worn for outdoor sports as well as for other occasions, is employed in this overblouse; the feature of which is the hand-embroidery in colored wool. Two pockets on the belt and the collar give it a most youthful appearance, no less than making it suitable for all types; in navy blue with Copenhagen and red embroidery, or black with white; sizes 34 to 44 . . . . $7.90

SMART FURS

*In the wearing of the fur scarf, there is
an interesting diversity always; the
illustrations, suggestive of modish ways,
are typical of the present modes.*

73F36 Scarf of black lynx, excellent
quality $45.00

73F37 Scarf of pointed fox (double
fur); in dark taupe, with white points; very
effective $38.00

73F38 Scarf of natural stone mar-
ten, made of two choice skins $60.00

73F39 Scarf of brown fox (double
fur). Exceptional value . $22.50

73F39A The Scarf quoted in
No. 73F39 is also obtainable in black or
dark taupe $22.50

73F40 Scarf of black fox; silk-lined.
Specially priced $28.00

73F40A The Scarf illustrated in
No. 73F40 is also obtainable in dark
taupe or brown $28.00

73F41 Scarf of natural stone mar-
ten, one skin, double fur of selected color
and quality; particularly smart for wear with
the tailleur $30.00

THE SEASON'S HATS

34F30 The use of leather is one of the new features on the autumn hats, and here it forms the petals of the flowers which are outlined with stitching on a hat of duvetyn; in sand-color, trimmed with brown, also brown trimmed with sand-color or black trimmed with Copenhagen blue **$8.00**

34F32 This Mushroom Shape is of duvetyn, with the brim somewhat modified front and back; the elaborate braid embroidery, in rather an individual pattern, is in silk; the colors include brown trimmed with sand-color, black trimmed with Copenhagen blue, also sand-color trimmed with navy blue **$9.75**

34F33 Of brown velvet, this Shape cuts in at the back and is faced with sand-color duvetyn; a long quill of brown leather gives a smart effect; also in black with Copenhagen blue facing, trimmed with black quill **$12.75**

34F34 Hat of purple velvet, rolled off the face, and trimmed with quill of shaded ostrich; also in brown trimmed with sand-color or all-black **$9.50**

34F35 This Hat with soft rolling brim is of gray velvet; the embroidery is in navy blue-and-silver; also in brown trimmed with sand-color or black trimmed with Copenhagen blue **$4.50**

34F36 This Mushroom Shape is of black velvet, faced with black taffeta; trimmed with black glycerined feather pompons **$11.50**

34F37 Black panne velvet, combined with royal blue Lyons velvet, makes a hat of charming lines, with brim rolling at the left side and trimmed with a large bow of the royal blue velvet; also in all-black **$12.00**

34F38 This Poke Shape of gray velvet rolls at the edge, is smartly corded and trimmed with a flat bow at the side; also in brown or black **$6.50**

34F39 Turban of poppy-red duvetyn, appliqued with gray silk flowers, with the foliage in gray metal threads; also in chestnut brown trimmed with pheasant color **$9.75**

34F40 This draped Turban is of black velvet, corded at intervals, and the visor is of black satin; two black pins ornament the front; also in brown or purple **$9.75**

34F41 This Tricorn is of black velvet, with black hackle breast, flecked with white **$12.75**

34F42 Draped Turban of velvet, a narrow brim, trimmed with ostrich feathers which extend over the crown and across the back; also in brown, black or purple **$14.50**

NOTE—A number of the Hats illustrated on this page are shown with the frocks elsewhere in this catalogue

WOMEN'S HOSIERY

Women's Hosiery, in the regular sizes, is obtainable from 8 to 10½;
the extra sizes range from 8½ to 10½

25F70   Women's Ribbed silk Hose, for street or sports wear ; in black-and-white, brown-and-tan, beige or gray ; per pair **$5.00**
25F71   Women's silk Hose ; in black, white and the fashionable colors ; medium weight, all silk ; per pair **$3.50**

25F72   Women's silk Hose ; in black, white, gray, brown or beige, with openwork clocks in a variety of designs (pattern may vary) ; per pair **$3.50**
25F72A Women's silk Hose ; in black, white and the wanted colors ; zephyr weight (*not illustrated*) ; per pair **$3.95**
25F73   Women's silk Hose ; in black or white, with four-inch lisle garter top, with openwork clocks ; per pair **$2.95**

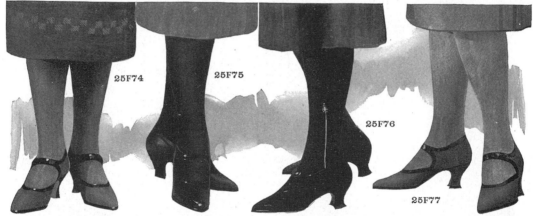

25F74   Women's silk Hose ; in black, white and the fashionable colors ; in a very durable all silk ; per pair **$2.75**
25F75   Women's silk Hose ; in black, white and the fashionable colors ; zephyr weight, all silk ; per pair **$2.75**

25F76   Women's silk Hose ; in black, white, African brown or gray, with embroidered clocks ; lisle tops and soles ; per pair . . . **$2.50**
25F77   Women's silk Hose ; in black, white and the fashionable colors ; lisle tops and soles. **Special**, per pair **$1.75**
25F77A Women's silk Hose , in white, black, African brown, gray or beige ; lisle tops, toes and heels (*not illustrated*) ; per pair . . **$1.00**

25F78   Women's novelty wool Hose ; in a variety of colorings (pattern may vary) ; per pair **$3.75**
25F79   Women's Knicker Hose, with novelty cuff tops (pattern may vary) ; in heather or Oxford ; per pair, **$3.25** and upward.

25F80   Women's ribbed wool Hose, with embroidered clocks ; in heather, gray or Lovat ; per pair **$3.50**
25F81   Women's wool Hose, with self-jacquard stripe ; in Lovat, heather, camel and black ; per pair **$2.50**

The Footwear shown on this and the following page is typical of the assortments for the current season, and is maintained in stock

FOR GIRLS AND JUNIOR MISSES

38F31 Hat of black plush cloth; trimmed with black fur ornaments at side **$2.75**

38F33 Hat of duvetyn, with rolled brim, trimmed with band of worsted around the crown, and finished with worsted ornaments at the side; in brown with sand-color or in navy blue with Copenhagen . **$3.75**

38F34 Hat of navy blue velvet; a mushroom shape, trimmed with two-toned plaited ribbon, in navy-blue-and-red, around the edge of brim, also an ornament of ribbon at side of the crown; also in black, trimmed with Copenhagen blue-and-black ribbon or beaver-color, trimmed with brown-and-sand-color ribbon; also shown on opposite page, with Coat model, No. 57F53 . . . . **$8.50**

38F35 Hat of cloth; a close-fitting rolled brim, slashed at the sides and trimmed with ornament at the front; in sand-color, brown or Copenhagen blue. This attractive little Hat is also shown with the two Coat models, Nos. 57F38 and 57F41, on this page **$2.75**

57F37 Slip-on Dress of checked wool homespun, with collar, vestee and cuffs of white linen; belt of leather; black tie; in tan or burgundy; sizes 6 to 14 years **$8.50**

57F38 Attractive Coat of an all-wool material, in navy blue or brown, in attractive mixture, with large collar buttoning high; inverted plait in the back; and detachable belt; sizes 6 to 12 years . .**$12.75**

57F39 Of soft all-wool diagonal material, in navy blue or tan, this Coat, is fashioned with set-in sleeves, inverted pockets, a double plait in back from yoke; a belted model; the becoming fur collar of Australian opossum; lined throughout with twilled sateen; sizes 6 to 10 years . . . **$19.75**

57F40 Slip-over Pantalette Frock of navy blue serge; hand-stitching forms the trimming; sizes 6 to 10 years **$9.85**

57F41 This smart model is developed in Bolivia, with collar of beaver, the back softly gathered from the yokeline; self-covered buttons, and a belt are interesting features; in Copenhagen blue or brown; lined throughout; sizes 6 to 10 years **$21.50**

57F42 Outer Coat of fine all-wool chinchilla, in new attractive shades, well tailored and of smart cut with wide belt, and lined throughout with twill sateen and interlined; in navy blue, French blue or cinnamon brown; sizes 6 to 12 years **$16.75**

57F43 Slip-on Frock of brown or black velveteen, without belt. The piping of contrasting color in crepe and the effective embroidery add to its smartness; 6 to 10 years **$15.50**

57F37 $8.50

38F31 $2.75

57F38 $12.75

57F39 $19.75

57F41 $21.50

38F33 $3.75

57F40 $9.85

57F42 $16.75

57F43 $15.50

38F34 $8.50

38F35 $2.75

SWEATER MODES AND ACCESSORIES;
ALSO BOUDOIR SACQUES

52F43 Women's and Misses' Boudoir Sacque of light-weight wool; in lavender-and-white, pink-and-white or all-white; sizes 36 to 44 . . . . **$3.90**

52F44 Women's and Misses' Silk Sweater, a Tuxedo model of novelty weave, fashioned with pockets and sash; in navy blue, brown or black; sizes 36 to 46 . . . . **$29.50**

52F45 Women's and Misses' Sweater of medium-weight, slightly brushed camel's hair, in the natural color; a Tuxedo model, with trimming of brown fiber; a decidedly new touch is the combination of wool and fiber in the double effect sash; also in black and white; sizes 36 to 46 . . . **$14.00**

52F46 Girls' Sweater of heavy-weight wool, with convertible collar; in brown or in navy blue; sizes 6 to 14 years **$6.25**

52F47 Girls' Tam o' Shanter of tan brushed camel's hair, also red or Copen. blue **$3.50**

52F48 Girls' Scarf of tan brushed camel's hair, also red or Copen. blue **$3.90**

52F49 Women's and Misses' Sweater Coat of medium-weight alpaca wool; in the natural brown shade with the contrast in tan; also in tan with brown; sizes 34 to 44 . . . . $10.50

52F50 Women's and Misses' Hat of tan camel's hair **$5.25**

52F51 Women's and Misses' Scarf of tan camel's hair—to complete the sports costume **$5.25**

52F52 Women's and Misses' wool Spencer, a surpliced style; in white, tan, black or gray; sizes 34 to 46 . . . . **$2.35**

52F53 Girls' Slip-on Sweater of mohair wool, a medium-weight; in tan with striped border in orange at bottom, or in navy blue with tan striped border; sizes 6 to 14 years **$4.90**

58F92 $8.50
58F94 $2.50
58F96 $2.50
58F98 $2.50
58F97 $15.50
58F100 $2.25
58F91 $22.50
58F93 $14.00
58F95 $12.75
58F102 $2.25
58F99 $9.75
58F101 $12.75
58F104 $2.75
58F105 $6.00 (Special)
58F103 $16.50
58F106 $7.50

For Wintry Days—Overcoats and Hats; also a Juniors' Norfolk Suit

Unless otherwise specified, Coat sizes range from 3 to 10 years; Hat sizes 6½ to 7

58F91 Overcoat of good quality warm material, with woolen lining, trimmed with collar of nutria; belt across back; in brown or olive heathers; sizes 3 to 8 only **$22.50**

58F92 Hat of brown or olive heather cloth, with slide-band of nutria that pulls over the ears **$8.50**

58F93 Overcoat of all-wool chinchilla, in cinnamon brown or navy blue. A woolen-lined garment with breast and side pockets; belt across back . . **$14.00**

58F94 Hat of cinnamon brown or navy blue chinchilla; silk lined **$2.50**

58F95 Overcoat of all-wool navy blue cloth, with gilt buttons and emblem on sleeve. A warm lining of red flannel; belt at back. A dressy, popular model **$12.75**

58F96 Hat of blue cloth, in the "Polo" style, with a band that can be pulled over the ears; silk lining . . . **$2.50**

58F97 Overcoat of gray or brown all-wool overcoating, in a stylish raglan model. The collar can be buttoned close or worn open; warm woolen lining. Inverted plait in back with belt all around **$15.50**

58F98 Hat of gray or brown cloth, in a smart model; silk-lined **$2.50**

58F99 Overcoat of all-wool brown or gray cloth; a double-breasted model, buttoned high; belt at back; warmly lined with a woolen material. Very specially priced at **$9.75**

58F100 Hat of brown or gray cloth; a smart model; well made; lined with silk **$2.25**

58F101 Overcoat of all-wool material in good-looking brown heathers; warmly lined with wool. A model that buttons high; breast and side pockets, belt across back, and plait down center **$12.75**

58F102 Hat of brown heather cloth, with band that pulls over the ears; silk-lined **$2.25**

58F103 Overcoat of all-wool gray or tan herring-bone cloth; a stylish raglan model, with belt; collar may be worn high; woolen-lined **$16.50**

58F104 Hat of gray or tan mixture; a closely-fitting shape **$2.75**
58F105 Sailor Suit of all-wool navy blue serge; a well-tailored model, featuring a new small sailor collar, with embroidered stars; regulation yoke and emblem; 3 to 10 yrs. Exceptional value at **$6.00**
58F106 Juniors' Norfolk Suit of brown corduroy; a well-tailored model with durable lining. An ideal school or play suit; 5 to 10 yrs. **$7.50**

INFANTS' APPAREL

49F351 Boys' Smock of blue or pink chambray, with collar and cuffs of white lawn; sizes 2 to 4 years . . . $2.85

49F352 Boys' Suit; trousers of tan or blue chambray; blouse of white poplin trimmed with hemstitching; sizes 2 to 5 years . . . $2.95

49F353 Boys' Suit of blue or maize chambray, with collar and cuffs of white poplin; sizes 2 to 4 years . . . $3.35

49F354 Suit of all-worsted navy blue jersey, with collar and cuffs of henna, trimmed with braid; emblem on sleeves; black silk tie; sizes 3 to 5 years . . . $6.00

49F355 Middy Suit of all worsted navy blue jersey, with collar and cuffs of henna, trimmed with braid and emblem on sleeve; sizes 3 to 5 years . . . $6.00

49F356 Middy Suit; blouse of white jean; trousers, collar and cuffs of blue cotton suiting trimmed with white braid; sizes 3 to 5 years . . . $2.85

49F356A Middy Suit; similar to No. 49F356, in the Oliver Twist style . . . $2.45

49F357 Boys' Suit; trousers of blue or green chambray, with blouse of white poplin; the frills on the collar and cuffs are picoted; sizes 2 to 5 years . $2.95

49F358 Boys' Suit; trousers of maize or helio Devonshire cloth; blouse of white poplin; hand-stitching; sizes 2 to 5 years . . $3.45

49F359 Boys' Suit of kiddie cloth, in blue or green; sizes 3 to 5 years . . . $1.90

49F360 Boys' Suit; trousers of blue or green chambray; blouse of white striped dimity; hand-smocking; also in all-white with blue smocking; sizes 2 to 5 years . $3.75

49F361 Bloomer-dress of red-and-white or lavender-and-white checked gingham, with collar and cuffs of white organdie; hand-stitching; 2 to 5 years $3.75

49F362 Bloomer-dress of blue or green linen, with piping of white linen; sizes 2 to 5 years $4.75

49F363 Bloomer-dress of green or pink chambray; collar, cuffs and trimming of white lawn, picoted; 2 to 5 years $4.10

49F364 Dress of blue crepe, trimmed with red; hand-stitching; 2 to 5 years $3.50

49F365 Bloomer-dress of pink-and-white or blue-and-white checked gingham; hand-stitching; 2 to 5 yrs $2.95

49F365A Bloomer-dress of blue chambray; similar to No. 49F365; hand-stitching; sizes 2 to 5 years . . . $2.95

49F366 Dress of all-worsted jersey, in combination of henna-and-gray or tan-and-blue; hand-stitching; 3 to 5 years . $7.50

49F367 Regulation Dress of fine-quality French serge; navy blue, with white braid; tie of red silk; 3 to 5 yrs. $6.75

49F367A Similar style to No. 49F367, in white jean with blue collar and cuffs; sizes 3 to 5 years $2.65

49F368 Dress of white crossbar dimity; hand-embroidered and hand-smocked in pink; sizes 2 to 5 years $3.65

49F369 Dress of imported white dotted Swiss; hand-smocked in rose color; sizes 2 to 5 years . . . $3.75

49F370 Dress of white poplin, with blue collar and cuffs; sizes 2 to 5 years $3.65

The "WARDROBE OF BABYHOOD," a complete brochure of Babies' Apparel, and Nursery Requirements, including Layettes, will be sent on request

62F31 $3.00
62F33 $3.00
62F59 $3.35
62F60 $3.75
62F35 $2.00
62F36 $8.00
62F30 $7.50
62F32 $7.50
62F40 $4.00
62F38 $2.25
62F34 $9.00
62F42 $3.10
62F44 $1.85
62F39 $12.85
62F37 $9.25
62F46 $1.50
62F48 $5.25
62F41 $11.50
62F43 $6.50
62F50 $3.75
62F45 $2.95
62F47 $18.00
62F52 $7.00
62F49 $14.25
62F61 $1.50
62F62 $1.50
62F51 $19.50
62F56 $2.50
62F53 $16.50
62F54 $5.25
62F63 $2.95
62F64 $2.00
62F58 $2.95
62F55 $9.75
62F57 $14.50

COATS AND HATS FOR JUVENILES

62F30 Coat of white crepe de Chine; hand-embroidered collar and cuffs; silk-lined; sizes 6 months to 2 years $7.50

62F31 Cap of white crepe de Chine; hand-scalloped; turn-back piece, lace edge; sizes infants' to 2 years $3.00

62F32 Coat of white wool cashmere; hand-embroidered collar and cuffs; silk-lined; sizes 6 months to 2 years $7.50

62F33 Cap of white silk poplin, with French knots and lace frills; sizes infants' to 2 years $3.00

62F34 Coat of white crepella; hand-embroidered collar and cuffs; silk-lined; sizes 6 months to 2 years $9.00

62F35 Cap of white bengaline silk; net frill; sizes infants' to 2 years . . . $2.00

62F36 Raincoat of rubberized cantonette with Hat to match; in tan or navy blue; sizes 2 to 5 years $8.00

62F37 Coat of polaire cloth (an all-wool material of soft mixture); in Copenhagen blue or tan. The lining is of sateen, and there is a belt at the back; sizes 1 to 4 years . . . $9.25

62F38 Hat of Copenhagen blue or tan polaire cloth, with ear tabs; matches Coat No. 62F37; sizes 1 to 4 years $2.25

62F39 Coat of tan polaire cloth, with inverted plait and belt at back; convertible collar; sizes 2 to 5 yrs. . $12.85

62F40 Hat of beaver, in black or brown; sizes 2 to 4 years $4.00

62F41 Coat of crepe de Chine; smocked, hand-stitched and silk-lined; in white or pink; 6 mos. to 2 yrs. $11.50

62F42 Cap of crepe de Chine; plaited frill, with lace edging; in white or pink; sizes infants' to 2 years $3.10

62F43 Coat of white chinchilla, with belt at back; unlined; sizes 1 to 2½ years . $6.50

62F44 Hat of white chinchilla; sizes 18 months to 3 years $1.85

62F45 Coat of white corduroy; unlined; sizes 6 months to 2 years $2.95

62F46 Hat of white corduroy; sizes 1 to 3 years $1.50

62F47 Coat of broadcloth, in tan or pink; beaver-trimmed, and made with belted back; silk-lined; sizes 18 months to 2½ years . . . $18.00

62F48 Polo Hat of broadcloth, in tan or pink; with beaver band; to match Coat No. 62F47; sizes 18 months to 2½ years $5.25

62F49 Coat of broadcloth, with smocked yoke; in henna or tan; trimmed with beaver; sizes 1 to 3 years $14.25

62F50 Corded Tam o' Shanter of broadcloth, in henna or tan, trimmed with nutria; matches Coat No. 62F49; sizes 1 to 3 years $3.75

62F51 Coat of soft brown veldet, a flare model, with collar of nutria; sizes 2 to 5 years $19.50

62F52 Hat of soft brown veldet, with nutria; matches Coat No. 62F51; sizes 2 to 5 years $7.00

62F53 Coat of French blue chinchilla, with belt at back and collar of wallaby fur. The lining is of sateen; sizes 2 to 5 years . . $16.50

62F54 Hat of French blue chinchilla, with band of wallaby fur; matches Coat No. 62F53; sizes 2 to 5 years $5.25

62F55 Coat of chinchilla, a belted model, in navy blue or cinnamon; 2 to 5 years $9.75

62F56 Polo Hat of chinchilla, in navy blue or cinnamon; matches Coat No. 62F55; sizes 2 to 5 years $2.50

62F57 Coat of Bolivia, in beaver shade, a flare model, with convertible collar. The lining is of sateen; sizes 3 to 5 years . . . $14.50

62F58 Hat of felt, in tan or brown, with quill trimming; sizes 3 to 5 years . . . $2.95

62F59 Bonnet of white silk poplin; shirred frill, edged with lace; sizes 6 months to 2½ years $3.35

62F60 Cap of white angora; swan's-down edging; sizes infants' to 1½ years $3.75

62F61 Cap of white corduroy, with silk ruche and turn-back piece; sizes infants' to 2 years $1.50

62F62 Cap of white crepe de Chine; shirred puffing; sizes infants' to 2 years $1.50

62F63 Boys' Hat of white silk poplin; button-trimmed; sizes 1 to 3 years . . $2.95

62F64 Cap of white crepe de Chine, with shirred frill; French knots; sizes infants' to 2 years $2.00

(Not Illustrated)

62F65 Quilted Coat Lining of white China silk; sizes 6 months to 2 years $3.00

62F66 Quilted Cap Lining of China silk; in pink, white or blue; sizes infants' to 2 years . . . . $ .55

70105 The beauty of crystal and rhinestone embroidery is seen in this imported evening gown of chiffon with flange drapery from the left shoulder. The embroidery appears also at the back, the design starting from the right shoulder; in orchid or gray; sizes 36 to 44 . . . . **$90.00**

70S106 The new cape effect, forming the sleeves, is seen in this model of georgette crepe. Two circular panels and a girdle showing rosettes with ornaments add to its charm; in green, navy blue or gray; sizes 36 to 40 . **$48.00**

70S107 A frock of charming simplicity, suitable for a bridesmaid. The material is of chiffon, in orchid, rose or white, and the flower at the side gives a girlish touch; sizes 38 and 40; also in 16 and 18 years **$42.50**

Here Are Engaging Gowns of Enticing Materials

70111 Chiffon and silver-metal lace: a shaped tunic is bordered with the lace, and the girdle has a feather ornament; in orchid or peach; sizes 34 to 40 only **$55.00**
70111A Same model may be specially ordered in fashionable high shades, for bridesmaids' costumes; 34 to 40 only **$55.00**
70112 Chenille brocaded crepe and feather trimming: this material is large-patterned and has a raised effect; the flange is of plain georgette; in sapphire blue, in which the brocaded pattern varies; sizes 34 to 44; size 46 may be specially ordered **$78.00**
70F113 Black lace and satin: the all-over lace pattern is filmy and falls softly, and the girdle of black satin has a novelty black ornament; sizes 34 to 44; size 46 may be specially ordered **$65.00**

6341
$110.00

6340
$138.00

6342
$115.00

Misses' Outer Coats

Fur-trimmed models; some untrimmed
A collection of highly individualized modes

Misses' coat sizes, unless otherwise specified, range as follows: 14 years, 32 inches bust, length 46 inches; 16 years, 34 inches bust, length 47 inches; 18 years, 36 inches bust, length 48 inches; 20 years equivalent to 38 inches bust, length 49 inches

NOTE— The Misses' coats illustrated may be specially ordered in sizes 38 to 44 bust, as indicated in the descriptions and are in average lengths, 49 to 50 inches.

6340 Evening wrap of royal blue chiffon velvet with natural Australian opossum; a luxuriously beautiful mode, with lining of crepe de Chine ; sizes 14, 16, 18 and 20 years; may also be specially ordered in sizes 38 to 44 bust **$138.00**
6340A The same model may be specially ordered in black, jade-green or American beauty **$138.00**
6341 Velnewvo and fur: collar, cuffs and border of nutria, with the shade of the all-wool material in Etruscan red or bark (fawn); lining of crepe de Chine; sizes 14, 16, 18 and 20 years; may also be specially ordered in sizes 38 to 44 bust **$110.00**
6341A The same model may be specially ordered in perfecto brown or balsam green, both models with nutria **$110.00**
6342 Of cuir de Laine (leather of wool), with fur collar and cuffs: in penny brown with beaver or black with squirrel ; lining of crepe de Chine; sizes 14, 16, 18 and 20 years; may also be specially ordered in 38 to 44 bust **$115.00**
6342A The same model may be specially ordered in Etruscan red or Lebanon green, both models with squirrel: also in viatka brown with beaver **$115.00**

Accessories from B. Altman & Co.

Boudoir Garments

55F31
$2.25

55F30
$1.10

72F34
$9.75

72F36
$21.50

72F35
$18.75

55F32
$1.45

72F37
$15.75

72F35
$25.00

55F30 Boudoir cap of blue, pink or lavender satin, daintily trimmed with lace and ribbon **$1.10**
55F31 Straight-line boudoir cap of blue, pink or lavender satin, trimmed with ruffled lace and buds . . . **$2.25**
55F32 Boudoir cap of white net, prettily trimmed with narrow blue, pink or lavender ribbon **$1.45**
72F34 Negligee of baronet satin: for practical wear; in French blue, coral or orchid; sizes 36 to 44 . . . . **$9.75**
72F34A The same model in crepe de Chine; in Copenhagen blue, peach or black **$11.75**
72F35 Negligee of miraline: trimmed with self-color marabou, and lined throughout with white China silk; in rose, Copenhagen or orchid; sizes 36 to 44 . **$18.75**
72F35A The same model in sizes, 46 to 50 **$22.50**
72F36 Negligee of satin meteor, trimmed with self-color silk-knotted fringe; in black, turquoise blue or coral; sizes 36 to 44 **$21.50**
72F37 Negligee of crepe de Chine: trimmed with real ecru Irish lace; in old rose or French blue; sizes 36 to 44 . **$15.75**
72F37A The same model as No. 72F37, lined with white albatross **$21.50**

72F38 Tea-gown: a beautiful slip-over model of pleated chiffon, under-bodice of self-color crepe de Chine, trimmed with silk lace, and sash of wide satin ribbon; in maize, peach or cornflower blue; sizes 36 to 44 . . . . **$25.00**

To facilitate the prompt and correct filling of orders, it is suggested that the order blank be used in every instance possible

58F101 Suit of worsted jersey, in tan with collar and trimming in an attractive brown contrast; sizes 4 to 8 years **$6.75**

58F102 Suit of worsted jersey, in regulation sailor style, with double yoke, emblem on sleeve, embroidered stars on collar; well tailored; in brown or tan; sizes 4 to 10 years **$6.75**

58F103 Middy suit; blouse of blue cotton suiting, emblem on sleeve; the collar and cuffs are of blue serge and made detachable, a great advantage in laundering; the trousers are of blue serge, lined; sizes 4 to 10 years . . . **$4.75**

58F103A The same model in a button-up style, the trousers buttoning to the blouse; sizes 3 to 8 years . **$4.75**

58F104 Attractive model of a finely-woven worsted jersey, a high-grade suit, well tailored; in tan with brown serge collar and cuffs; sizes 4 to 10 years . . . **$6.75**

58F105 Three-piece suit of all-wool gray tweed; the coat is mohair-lined and the trousers are lined; the vest of tweed has a detachable washable collar of white pique; sizes 6 to 10 years **$12.75**

58F105A The same model in blue serge . **$12.75**

58F106 Balkan model; blouse of tan linen crash, trousers of all-wool tan tweed, lined; sizes 3 to 9 years **$3.75**

58F107 Balkan model; blouse of white cotton gabardine; with detachable blue serge collar and cuffs, the trousers are of blue serge; sizes 3 to 9 years **$6.00**

58F108 Suit; blouse of pure tan linen with three rows of braid, emblem on sleeve, cord and whistle; trousers (which button to blouse) are of brown corduroy and lined; sizes 3 to 9 years **$2.95**

58F109 Suit of jersey; this popular style is adapted from the English middy, and is made of a substantial worsted jersey, in Copenhagen blue or tan; sizes 4 to 10 years; special at **$5.50**

To facilitate the prompt and correct filling of orders, it is suggested that the order blank be used in every instance possible. Additional order blanks will be sent on request

57S181 A bloomer frock of cotton print; the cuffs, bands and pockets are of plain color broadcloth and there are touches of hand-embroidery; in red or brown; sizes 6 to 10 years **$5.25**

57S182 Pongee and taffeta are used for this charming bloomer frock; the frock is of the natural tan pongee, while the trimmings are of the brown taffeta; sizes 6 to 10 years **$6.75**

57S183 Bloomer dress of checked gingham, with trimming of plain color chambray, touches of hand-embroidery, and a tie sash at either side; in lavender or green; sizes 6 to 10 years . . . **$2.95**

57S184 This loose-hanging frock with bloomers, is made of Copenhagen blue or brown chambray, while the collar, cuffs and piping are of white repp; hand-stitching; sizes 6 to 10 years . . **$1.85**

57S185 Wool jersey is used in this charming little bloomer frock; stitched with silk floss; in henna or tan; sizes 6 to 10 years . **$7.25**

57S186 Striped and plain broadcloth are used in this charming one-piece frock; the waist is button-trimmed and the skirt is pleated; in Copenhagen blue or brown; 8 to 14 years . . **$5.50**

57S181 $5.25

57S182 $6.75

57S183 $2.95

57S184 $1.85

57S185 $7.25

57S186 $5.50

57S187 $5.25

57S188 $3.50

57S187 Dress of lavender or brown ramie linen, with the popular drawnwork; the collar and cuffs are of white linen, finished with a lace edging; sizes 8 to 14 years **$5.25**

57S188 One-piece dress of striped cotton material; the inverted pleats down either side of front are trimmed with pearl buttons and the collar and cuffs are of white pique finished with a lace edging; sizes 10 to 16 years; white stripes on green or brown ground . . **$3.50**

The Two-piece Tailleur and Ensemble, which consider the slender type and the woman of more stately proportions

69S35 Imported tweed of very fine quality combined with superb tailoring insure a comfortable feeling of being well-dressed in this two-piece suit, with a single-breasted hipline coat and mannish notched collar. The coat lining is of soft-quality satin; in gray or brown mixture; sizes 34 to 44; may also be specially ordered in sizes 16 and 18 years **$39.50**

69S36 Twill cord, an all-wool fabric of great popularity, is employed in this two-piece model, with three-quarter-length coat, made in the double-breasted style, with inverted pockets at the hipline, and rounded cuffs. The skirt is a wrap-around model. The tailored details will be particularly noted; coat lining of a superior quality of crepe; in navy or Oxford gray; sizes 34 to 44 . . . . . . **$50.00**

69S36A The same model may be specially ordered in black **$50.00**

69S37 Flannels contribute smartly to the Spring mode, and particularly smart is this two-piece box-coat model of a very superior quality. The skirt is an improved wrap-around model, which has darts over the hips. The tailoring is exceptional; in biscuit-color, powder blue or white; sizes 34 to 44; may also be specially ordered in size 16 18 years **$35.00**

6938 For the woman of large proportions, an extremely satisfactory ensemble suit is shown in twill-bloom with frock of satin-back crepe. New points of the vogue are followed and emphasis put on slenderizing effects; in snuff-brown or navy; sizes 38½ to 46½ **$85.00**

6938A The same model may be specially ordered in all-black **$85.00**

6938B These models may be specially ordered in sizes 48½ to 52½ **$85.00**

6938
$85.00

69S35
$39.50

69S36
$50.00

69S37
$35.00

The smartest and most effective of accessories—a fox scarf is shown with the Tailleur No. 69S36. It is typical of the furs which may be obtained for the Spring season

Unless otherwise specified, Women's Tailored Suits are in sizes 34 to 44; size 46 may be specially ordered

Youthful Blouses and Sweaters: Shown Variously with New Skirt Models

52S113 Sports skirt of striped homespun, in combination pleats; in Copenhagen blue with rust or tan with green and orange; sizes 14, 16, 18 and 20 years **$5.90**

54S116 This sports overblouse is developed in flannel, trim and smart; in natural tan, Formosa (new light rust), grass green, white or matelot (the new blue); sizes 14, 16, 18 and 20 years; also in sizes 40 and 42 bust **$11.75**

54S117 The "Peter Pan" tucked bosom appears here in an extremely late mode in overblouses; the material a crepe de Chine; in white, Formosa (new light rust), matelot or Spanish red; sizes 34 to 42 . **$11.50**

54S118 Peasant style overblouse of crepe de Chine, with embroidery in contrasting colors; in white, matelot (the new French blue), Spanish red, navy or orange blossom (the new yellow); sizes 14, 16, 18 and 20 years; also in size 40 bust **$11.90**

54S119 Slip-over sweater of heavy wool, with the turtle neckline; navy blue or white; sizes 34 to 42 . . . **$8.75**

54S120 Slip-over "Peter Pan" sweater of silver-tone yarn; maize, lanvin green or white; 34 to 42 **$9.75**

54S119
$8.75

54S120
$9.75

52S113
$5.90

54S117
$11.50

54S116
$11.75

52S112
$12.75

54S118
$11.90

52S114
$12.50

52S111
$6.75

52S115
$12.50

52S114 Pleated skirt of wool plaid; in tan or gold with smart contrasting colors introduced in the plaid effect; sizes 14, 16, 18 and 20 yrs. **$12.50**

52S114A Same model in plain-color flannel; white, tan, gray, green or lipstick red **$11.50**

52S112 Skirt of flat crepe; gracefully pleated; new panel front and plain back; in white, crab apple, pigtail blue, navy or fallow; sizes 14, 16, 18 and 20 years **$12.75**

52S115 A desirable model is shown here in this slip-on skirt of flannel, cut with shoulder extension, and having a cluster of small box-pleats in front, and two slashed pockets; in Piping Rock, pumpkin, apple green, scarlet, silver gray or white; sizes 14, 16, 18 and 20 years **$12.50**

52S111 Well-tailored flannel skirt in a wrap style, with an inverted pleat, trimmed with small buttons; in gray, tan, green or powder blue; sizes 14, 16, 18 and 20 years **$6.75**

34S212
$9.75

34S213
$4.75

34S214
$9.00

34S215
$9.00

34S216
$9.50

34S219
$8.75

34S218
$4.50

34S217
$10.50

34S220
$9.75

Fashionable Millinery

34S212 Small poke-shape of taffeta, with sectional crown and rows of straw grass trimming on side; in red, Copenhagen blue or navy **$9.75**

34S213 Large taffeta hat, with folds of horse-hair on brim, cockade of ribbon on side; navy or black **$4.75**

34S214 Soft hat of Roman striped ribbon, with hemp brim; fringe effect on side; with facing in red or navy **$9.00**

34S215 Hat of Bangkok straw, with soft draping around crown; in black, navy or white **$9.00**

34S216 Hat of crepe de Chine; slightly rolled, with high crown; roses on top; Copenhagen blue or lanvin green **$9.50**

34S217 Brimmed hat of split straw, with soft horse-hair trimming around crown and flowers on side; navy or black **$10.50**

34S218 Medium-size mushroom shape of crepe de Chine; hemp crown; cockade on side; in red crown with black brim; all-white or all-tan . **$4.50**

34S219 Small hat of faille-and-straw combination, with bow on top of crown; in red, Copenhagen blue or gray **$8.75**

34S220 New rolled hat of taffeta, with straw binding; grosgrain ribbon around crown and bow at back; in brown-and-sand or all-navy . . **$9.75**

34S201
$6.75

34S200
$9.75

34S202
$7.50

34S203
$5.25

34S206
$10.50

34S204
$9.00

34S205
$5.25

34S207
$10.50

34S208
$9.75

Fashionable Millinery

34S200 Short-back poke-shape of hemp, with flower trimming around crown and gold ribbon ; in navy or henna **$9.75**

34S201 Small hat of crepe de Chine; short back; flat flower trimming across front ; in white or henna **$6.75**

34S202 Medium-size leghorn; rolled at back, in the natural shade; trimmed with royal blue, white or black **$7.50**

34S203 Soft-rolled brim hat of felt; cut off in back; felt loops on side ; in cherry, white, sand or almond **$5.25**

34S204 Turban of Milan hemp ; in navy or black; trimmed with Roman striped ribbon **$9.00**

34S205 Crushable felt hat ; with rows of cut-edge felt, moire band and cockade at side; in jade, white, rose or yellow . **$5.25**

34S206 Soft rolled silk hat; rolled all around; Tagal straw facing, with tailored bow on side; in white, cocoa or navy **$10.50**

34S207 Matron's hat of moire and draped horse-hair braid around crown; small brim; pin in front; in black, brown or navy . **$10.50**

34S208 Medium-size dress hat of horse-hair, with high flower trimming at back ; velvet binding; in black, with colored flower, or in all-red **$9.75**

Apart from the habits featured in the catalogue, other models are in stock; imported whipcords, bedford cord and meltons; also assortments of novelty linens; the three-piece knicker suit in tweed is also a special feature.

NOTE—A measurement blank for ordering Riding Apparel appears on page 129. By following the instructions contained in this guide, great assistance will be given in the selection of the required size.

52S30 Sleeveless riding coat, slender lines; of fine quality flannel; red, green, brown, tan, rust or black; 34 to 42 bust; also 14 to 18 years **$14.50**

52S30
$14.50

52S31
$8.50

52S36
$3.75

52S32
$15.75

52S33
52S33A
$16.75

54S38
$5.00

52S34
$5.95

52S35
$14.50

Footwear and accessories from B. Altman & Co.

The Riding Habits, Separate Breeches, Knickers and Knicker Suits quoted are custom-made in B. Altman & Co.'s own workrooms. Women's Riding Habits are in sizes 34 to 42 inches bust; Misses' Riding Habits are in sizes 14, 16 and 18 years; Junior sizes 13, 15 and 17 years; Children's Riding Habits are in sizes 8 to 14 years. Women's size 44 may be specially ordered, a few days being required to fill orders. Cloth habits are lined with serge and faced with rubber; breeches reinforced with buckskin.

52S31 Riding breeches of checked linen; in black-and-white or brown-and-white; sizes 26 to 34 in. waist **$8.50**

52S31A Separate breeches of white linen; finest quality; sizes 26 to 34 in. waist **$9.50**

52S31B Separate breeches of tan linen; same as above **$8.00**

52S32 Junior misses' riding habit of tan linen; cut on straight lines, featuring the new pocket; sizes 13, 15 and 17 years . . . **$15.75**

52S32A The same model may be specially ordered in the sleeveless style . . **$14.75**

52S32B Children's riding habit of tan linen; the same fine-quality straight-line coat as No. 52S32; sizes 8, 10 and 12 years **$14.50**

52S33 Riding habit of tan linen; superior quality workmanship, 34 to 42 bust; also 14 to 18 yrs.; special, **$16.75**

52S33A Same model in size 44 **$16.75**

52S33B Same model as 52S33; sleeveless **$15.75**

52S33C Riding habit, finest quality white linen; tailoring in same style as 52S32 **$25.00**

52S33D Same as above, with sleeveless coat; 34 to 44 bust; also 14 to 18 years . **$22.50**

52S34 Separate knickers of plaid linen; in tan-and-brown; 26 to 34 inches waist **$5.95**

52S35 Knicker suit; tweed; coat unlined and sleeveless; the newest tweed in tan or gray mixture; fine plaid design; 34 to 40 bust; also 14 to 18 yrs. **$14.50**

52S35A Separate wrap-around skirt; same materials as No. 52S35 may be specially ordered; sizes 26 to 34 waist **$7.50**

52S36 Rustproof English spurs; metal; blk. or russet straps **$3.75**

52S37 Vests of fine-quality flannel, correct riding colors; green, red or tan; trim. with brass buttons; 34 to 42 bust; also 14 to 18 years (not illustrated) . . **$7.50**

52S39 Riding habit; whipcord; all-brown or contrasting breeches in tan; also brown heather mixture; misses' 14 to 18, women's 34 to 44 (not illus.) . **$49.50**

54S38 Sports Shirt; 34 to 42; in white, tan or French blue; English broadcloth, **$5.00**; radium silk . . **$9.75**

14S28 Windsor tie of crepe de Chine; in navy, red, brown, Copen., orange or black; worn with blouse No. 54S38 $ **.45**

78S31 Rubber cap; in an assortment of colors . . . . $ .50

78S35 Bathing hat of rubberized satin; in black, Copenhagen
blue, red, green or purple $3.75

78S31
50¢

78S37 Rubber
cap; an assortment
of colors . $ .65

78S35
$3.75

78S37
65¢

78S49 Rubber
cap; in an assort-
ment of designs and
colors . . $ .45

78S49
45¢

78S30
$4.50

78S48
$1.95

78S32
75¢

78S33
$5.50

78S34
$4.90

78S36
$8.25

78S46
90¢

78S39
45¢

78S42
75¢

78S45
$3.25

78S47
90¢

78S38
$4.50

78S41
$9.75

78S40
95¢

78S44
$1.75

78S43
$1.95

78S47
90¢

78S43 Slippers of black
satin; one button; sizes 3,
4, 5, 6 and 7; per pair
$1.95

78S44 Hand - painted
rubber bag; in black only,
with harmonious decora-
tions $1.75

BATHING AND
BEACH
COSTUMES AND ACCESSORIES

78S30 Misses' one-piece swimming suit of wool
jersey, in a novelty knitted weave; in red, Copenhagen
blue or black; sizes 16, 18 and 20 years . . . $4.50

78S32 Slippers of black canvas; sizes 3, 4, 5, 6 and
7; per pair . . . . $ .75

78S33 Women's one-piece swimming suit of wool
jersey; rib-knit; in black, red, royal blue or green;
sizes 36 to 44 . . . . $5.50

78S33A The same model in black only; size 46 . $6.50

78S34 Beach cape of Roman striped toweling . $4.90

78S36 Women's one-piece swimming suit of wool jersey
in novelty stripes; in black-and-white or Copenhagen blue-
and-white; sizes 36 to 44 . . . . $8.25

78S38 Women's bathing suit of surf cloth, with pipings
of pique; in black with white, black with Copenhagen blue
or in all-black; sizes 36 to 44 . . . . $4.50

78S38A The same model in extra size, 46 . . . $6.50

78S39 Diving cap of heavy rubber; in black, red or white
$ .45

78S40 Rubber slippers, in moire finish; in Copenhagen
blue, red or black; sizes 4, 5, 6 and 7; per pair . . $ .95

78S41 Women's bathing suit of black taffeta, with pipings of
contrasting color; in black with red, black with Copenhagen blue
or black with white; sizes 36 to 44 . . . . . . $9.75

78S41A The same model in black poplin, with contrasts as
noted $7.50

78S42 Rubber cap; an assortment of colors . . . $ .75

78S45 Junior misses' one-piece swimming suit of wool jersey;
in red or Copenhagen; sizes 8, 10, 12, 14 and 16 years $3.25

78S46 Rubber cap; in an assortment of colors . . $ .90

78S47 Rubber slippers, in the moire finish; in red or Copenhagen blue; sizes 11, 12 and 13 years; per pair . . $ .90

78S48 Children's one-piece suit of wool jersey; in Copenhagen blue, red or navy; sizes 2, 4 and 6 years . . . $1.95

(Not Illustrated)

78S52 Cotton combination; in black; sizes 36 to 46 $ .90

78S53 Wool combination; in black; sizes 36 to 46 . $3.00

78S54 Glove silk combination; in black; sizes 36 to 46 $5.00

78S55 Silk combination; in black; sizes 36 to 46 . $7.50

Silk
Undergarments

79S160 Nightrobe of crepe de Chine ; a youthful style ; the points are finished with a picot edge ; in pink or peach-color ; sizes 14, 15 and 16 inches **$6.90**

79S161 Tailored nightrobe of crepe de Chine ; trimmed with hemstitching ; in pink, orchid or peach-color ; sizes 14, 15 and 16 inches **$7.95**

79S162 Nightrobe of crepe de Chine; trimmed with hand-made crochet lace, Valenciennes edging and pin tucks; in pink or peach-color ; sizes 14, 15 and 16 inches **$8.75**

79S163 Nightrobe of crepe de Chine; trimmed with Valenciennes lace and hand-made crochet; in pink or orchid ; sizes 14, 15 and 16 inches **$4.95**

79S164 Nightrobe of crepe de Chine ; a V-neck model ; trimmed with filet lace ; in pink; sizes 14, 15 and 16 inches **$8.50**

79S165 Nightrobe of trousseau crepe ; a square-neck model ; trimmed with a pretty pattern of lace, outlined with feather-stitching ; ribbon belt ; in pink, Nile green or peach-color ; sizes 14, 15 and 16 inches **$10.75**

79S166 The dainty dansant set shown on the figure in the panel comprises step-in drawer, bandeau-brassiere and garters to match ; the material is crepe de Chine, in pink, peach-color or Nile, trimmed with lace ; this is designed not only for the uncorseted figure, but may also be worn over the corset; bandeau 36 to 40 inches bust; drawer lengths 21 and 23 inches; the set **$7.50**

79S167 Step-in chemise of heavy-quality crepe de Chine ; trimmed with embroidered net and Valenciennes lace ; in pink, peach-color or orchid ; sizes 36 to 44 . . . . **$5.75**

*Fasso Corsets;
also other Corset
Models Designed
by Expert
Corsetieres*

45S150 Fasso corset of pink broche;
low at top; long, straight hipline, trimmed
with ribbon and lace; hook and eye below
front steel; two pairs of hose supporters
attached; sizes 24 to 32 **$10.75**

45S151 Non-lacing corset of pink broche, combined with firm
elastic; low at top; long, straight hip and very flat at back; two
pairs of hose supporters are attached; sizes 26 to 36 . . . **$5.00**

45S153 Corset of pink batiste; low at top, medium length at
bottom; hook and eye below front steel; three pairs of hose supporters are attached; sizes 22 to 32 . . . . **$4.25**

45S154 Non-lacing corset of pink broche; elastic at sides; lightly
boned; hook and eye below front steel; two pairs of hose supporters
are attached; sizes 24 to 32 . . . . **$2.00**

45S152 Non-lacing corset of pink
broche, with sections of firm elastic;
low at top, long hip, very flat at back,
hooks and eyes below front steel; three
pairs of hose supporters are attached;
sizes 26 to 36 . . . . . . **$6.00**

45S155 Non-lacing corset of pink
broche, with sections of elastic; low at
top, long hip, very flat at back, boned at
front and back only, hooks and eyes
below front steel; four pairs of hose supporters are attached; 26 to 36 **$7.25**

45S156 Corset of pink broche; low at top, with elastic insert at bust; front
a little higher to hold diaphragm; hook and eye, also eyelets, below front steel;
three pairs of hose supporters are attached; sizes 23 to 32 . . . . **$7.50**

*Fasso Corsets, made in France, exclusive to B. Altman & Co., are developed
in different materials, and are, admittedly, the most successful corset that
has ever been introduced in the American market. Other French models may
also be selected, from the short belt to the regulation style, as well as elastic
enveloppantes and elastic slip-on corsets, which lace at the back; also a large
assortment of lace and embroidered linen brassieres. Estimates will be given
for corsets made to order; accurate and comprehensive measurements
should be supplied. Upon request, prices will also be given for copying corset
models furnished by patrons.*

LITTLE BOYS' AND GIRLS' SUITS

49S642 Boys' suit of brown or blue Peggy cloth; white collar and cuffs; edged with white frills; sizes 2 to 5 years. **$2.25**

49S643 Boys' suit; trousers of blue or green Peggy cloth; blouse of white crossbar dimity; collar and cuffs edged with ruffles; sizes 2 to 5 years **$2.25**

49S644 Boys' suit of blue or green Peggy cloth; white collar and cuffs; hand-stitching; sizes 2 to 5 years **$1.60**

49S645 Boys' suit of brown or green Peggy cloth; collar and cuffs of white, edged in color to match the suit; sizes 2 to 5 years **$2.10**

49S646 Boys' suit; trousers of blue or maize chambray, blouse of fine white broadcloth; hand-smocking in color to match trousers; sizes 2 to 5 years **$2.85**

49S647 Boys' suit; trousers of blue or maize Devonshire, blouse of white striped dimity; sizes 2 to 5 years **$3.00**

49S648 Boys' suit; trousers, collar and cuffs of blue or green Peggy cloth, blouse of white poplin; hand-smocking; sizes 2 to 5 years **$1.75**

49S649 Boys' suit; trousers of blue or maize chambray, blouse of white crossbar dimity; hand-smocking and stitching; sizes 2 to 5 years **$3.25**

49S650 Boys' suit of maize or green chambray; collar and cuffs of fine white broadcloth; hand-smocking; 2 to 4 yrs. **$2.95**

49S650A Similar style to No. 49S650; all-white imported English broadcloth; sizes 2 to 4 years **$2.85**

49S651 Boys' suit of lavender or green Devonshire; blouse of fine white broadcloth; sizes 2 to 5 years **$3.35**

49S652 Boys' suit of rose or maize Devonshire; collar, cuffs and vestee of white organdie; sizes 2 to 4 years . . . **$2.95**

49S653 Boys' suit of tan or blue Devonshire; collar and cuffs of fine white broadcloth; hand-stitching; sizes 2 to 5 years **$3.75**

49S654 Boys' suit of white jean; collar and cuffs of blue, trimmed with white; sizes 2 to 5 years **$2.25**

49S655 Boys' suit of khaki-colored jean; sizes 2 to 5 years **$1.75**

49S655A Girls' khaki suit, consisting of bloomers attached to a white underwaist and middy blouse; sizes 3 years to 5+. (See note on page 81) **$1.25**

49S656 Boys' suit of blue or green Peggy cloth; collar and cuffs of white pique; sizes 2 to 4 years **$1.50**

49S657 Boys' suit of maize or lavender chambray; embroidered collar and cuffs; sizes 2 to 5 years **$2.00**

A number of the little models illustrated are in 5+, an intermediate size, larger than five, and smaller than the regular six

49S682 Dress of white imported dotted Swiss, with blue dots;
collar, cuffs and panel of blue lawn; lace-trimmed; 2 to 5+ **$4.10**

49S684 Bloomer-dress of green or blue print; white collar and
cuffs; sizes 2 years to 5+ **$2.10**

49S685 Dress; peach or green imported voile; collar, cuffs, pleating
of white voile; hemstitched in color to match dress; 2 to 5 . **$2.95**

49S687 Bloomer-dress of maize or blue shadow lawn; hand-embroidery; trimmed with picoted ruffles; sizes 2 years to 5+   **$2.85**

49S688 Bloomer-dress of peach or lavender print; pleated ruffle
around neck, and cuffs of white lawn edged with hand-made picot;
hand-stitching; sizes 2 years to 5+ **$3.35**

49S690 Dress of henna or blue dotted lawn; trimmed with white
picoted ruffles; hand-stitching; sizes 2 years to 5+ . . . **$3.25**

49S692 Bloomer-dress of peach or green voile; hand-stitching;
with ruffles, picoted to match color of dress; sizes 2 to 5+ **$2.95**

49S693 Bloomer-dress of blue or lavender printed lawn; hand-
smocking; sizes 2 years to 5+ **$2.90**

49S694 Dress of tangerine or pink striped voile; hand-smocking; collar and cuffs of tan voile; sizes 2 years to 5+ . . **$2.00**

49S695 Bloomer-dress of maize-and-white or blue-and-white
striped sateen; collar and cuffs of white sateen; hand-smocking; sizes
2 years to 5+ **$3.75**

49S696 Bloomer-dress of green-and-white or maize-and-white
checked lawn; hand-smocking; sizes 2 years to 5+ . . . **$2.95**

49S697 Bloomer-dress of green or lavender print; white collar,
vestee and pocket tops edged with hand-made picot; 2 to 5+ **$2.95**

49S698 Bloomer-dress of green or maize chambray; white collar
and trimming; sizes 2 years to 5+ **$1.95**

49S699 Dress of white lawn, with red or green dots; white collar
and cuffs; hand-smocking; sizes 2 years to 5+ **$2.50**

49S700 Bloomer-dress of blue-and-white or rose-and-white sateen;
collar and cuffs of white sateen; hand-stitching; 2 to 5+ . **$3.35**

49S702 Bloomer-dress of maize or blue checked gingham; hand-
smocking and hand-embroidery; collar and cuffs of soisette to match
color of check; sizes 2 years to 5+ **$2.65**

49S703 Bloomer-dress of pink or green chambray; hand-smocking
and stitching; sizes 2 years to 5+ **$2.95**

62S683 Hat, white organdie; pink or blue ribbon; 2 to 5 **$2.95**

62S686 Hat of pink or white organdie; sizes 2 to 4 years **$1.90**

62S689 Hat of peanut straw; navy or green ribbon; 2 to 4 **$2.95**

62S691 Hat of white organdie; with blue or pink ribbon trimming;
sizes 2 to 4 years **$2.95**

62S701 Organdie sun bonnet; white or pink; 6 months to 2 years
$1.45

(Not Illustrated)

62S705 Cap lining of silk; in pink, white or blue; sizes infants'
to 2 years . . . . **$ .50**

62S706 Coat of white corduroy; unlined; 1 and 2 years **$3.50**

Very Feminine Are These Lace=trimmed Negligees of Silk

55S120 Straight-line boudoir cap of net, trimmed with blue, pink or lavender ribbon **$1.10**

55S121 Boudoir cap of satin and net, trimmed with blue, pink or lavender ribbon ruffles **$2.25**

55S122 Boudoir cap of blue, pink or lavender satin, trimmed with ribbon and lace **$1.45**

72S125 Negligee of crepe de Chine, is effectively trimmed with ruffles of self-material; in rose, turquoise blue or black; sizes 36 to 44 . . . . **$11.90**

72S125A Same model as No. 72S125 in extra sizes 46, 48, 50 and 52 . . . . **$13.50**

72S126 Negligee of crepe de Chine, featuring the new cape effect; in Copen blue, rose or black; sizes 36 to 44 . . . . **$16.50**

72S127 Breakfast coat of chiffon taffeta, daintily trimmed with Valenciennes lace; in French blue, orchid or coral; sizes 36 to 44 . . . . **$15.00**

72S128 Breakfast coat of radium silk with collar, sleeves and pockets charmingly trimmed with self-color frills; in orchid, Copen or coral; sizes 36 to 44 **$7.85**

72S129 Negligee of crepe de Chine with collar, cuffs and pockets trimmed with embroidered net and Valenciennes lace; loose panels of crepe de Chine are also lace-trimmed; in pink, orchid or turquoise blue; sizes 36 to 44 . . . . **$19.75**

55S120
$1.10

72S125
$11.90

55S122
$1.45

55S121
$2.25

72S126
$16.50

72S127
$15.00

72S128
$7.85

72S129
$19.75

Breakfast Coats in New Styles and Fabrics

72S135 Negligee of superior quality satin with attractive pointed lower edge and sleeves, finished with novelty edging; smart velvet motif trims the pocket; in French blue, orchid, bois de rose, gloria (rose) or black; sizes 36 to 44 . **$18.75**

72S136 Breakfast coat of a new cotton and silk figured crepe, trimmed with self-color frills; in rose, Copen or black background; sizes 36 to 44 . **$12.50**

72S137 Breakfast coat of figured rayon trimmed with contrasting satin ribbon; belt of self-material; in tan or blue predominating; sizes 36 to 44 . . . **$8.90**

72S138 Robe of albatross with set-in sleeves and front in tuxedo effect; fronts, pockets and cuffs are trimmed with self-color hand-stitching; in French blue, rose or lavender; sizes 36 to 44 . . . . **$10.75**

72S139 Negligee of colored cotton voile, a side-tie model attractively trimmed with dainty Valenciennes lace; in French blue, coral or lavender; sizes 36 to 44 **$6.90**

55S131 Straight-line boudoir cap of lace with elastic at back, and blue, pink or lavender ribbon crossing crown **$2.25**

55S132 Boudoir cap of net, trimmed with lace and blue, pink or lavender ribbon **$1.25**

55S133 Boudoir cap of blue, pink or lavender satin, trimmed with ribbon and lace **$1.10**

To facilitate the prompt and correct filling of orders, it is suggested that the order blank be used in every instance possible. Additional order blanks will be sent on request.

55S131
$2.25

55S132
$1.25

72S135
$18.75

72S136
$12.50

72S137
$8.90

72S138
$10.75

55S133
$1.10

72S139
$6.90

Brassiere and Corset Combinations

45S65 Combination garment, consisting of bandeau of pink batiste, hip confiner of batiste, with elastic sections, and step-ins of rayon; all in one garment; fastens at side with hooks and eyes; two pairs of hose supporters attached; sizes 32 to 40 (to be ordered according to bust measure) $5.00

45S66 Corset and brassiere combination of firm pink figured batiste; long model; elastic section on hips; front and underarms of brassiere made of silk-finished tricot; brassiere reinforced over front to hold figure firmly; hooks at side of front; three pairs of hose supporters attached; sizes 32 to 48 (to be ordered according to bust measure) $4.00

45S67 Corset and brassiere combination of pink batiste suitable for the miss; top of silk-finished tricot; elastic at side of hip; hooks at side of front; two pairs of hose supporters attached; sizes 32 to 38 (to be ordered according to bust measure) $3.00

45S68 Corset and brassiere combination of firm pink broche; long model with surgical elastic gores at hips; boned across front and at back to hold figure firmly; hooks at side of front; narrow lace edge at top; three pairs of hose supporters attached; sizes 34 to 48 (to be ordered according to bust measure) $5.50

45S69 Corset and brassiere combination of pink striped batiste; long model with elastic gore at side; boned at center front to hold figure firmly; hooks at side of front; two pairs of hose supporters attached; sizes 32 to 48 (to be ordered according to bust measure) $2.00

45S65
$5.00

45S67
$3.00

45S69
$2.00

45S68
$5.50

45S66
$4.00

45S71
75¢

45S70
$1.50

45S72
$2.50

45S73
$2.00

45S74
$1.00

45S70 Hip confiner of pink figured batiste with elastic at sides; boned across front only; suitable for the miss; two pairs of hose supporters attached; sizes 25 to 32 . . . . $1.50

45S71 Bandeau to match hip confiner No. 45S70, narrow lace edge at top; shoulder straps of ribbon; sizes 30 to 38 . . . . . . $ .75

45S72 Bandeau of fine white lace, with shoulder straps of pink ribbon and dainty flower at front; hooks and eyes at back; sizes 32 to 38 $2.50

45S73 Brassiere of white linen; long model with elastic gore at bottom, shoulder straps of ribbon; narrow lace edge at top; hooks and eyes at back; sizes 32 to 46 . . . . $2.00

45S74 Brassiere of pink figured cotton material with elastic gore at bottom; hooks and eyes at back; tape shoulder straps; sizes 32 to 46 . . . . $1.00

Flaring Tunics and Scalloped Tiers Are Smart

70S110 Flowered chiffon and beaded banding make a charming afternoon frock, trimmed with contrasting ribbon; slip of satin; in white-and-black, or rose, blue-and-tan combination; pattern may vary; sizes 34 to 44 **$58.00**

70S111 Figured silk crepe develops this frock, and fine lace supplies the trimming; scalloped panels at side form pockets; in tan-and-green, blue-and-red, white-and-red printed design; pattern may vary; sizes 34 to 44 . . . . **$45.00**

70S111A Same style as No. 70S111, in navy-and-white polka dotted silk crepe **$45.00**

70S110
$58.00

70S111
$45.00

34S120
$7.50

70S112 Georgette frock over a slip of self material, with tucked front; front of skirt is circular; convertible collar, in tan, gray, navy or all-black; sizes 34 to 44 (may be specially ordered in size 46) **$29.75**

70S113 Frock of faille crepe follows the vogue for scallops; convertible neck with vestee, collar and cuffs of flesh georgette, in black or navy; sizes 34 to 44 . . . . **$48.00**

34S120 Dress hat of horsehair, rolled at back, flowers across front, taffeta flange, Italian blue (Copen) or navy with colored flowers . . **$7.50**

70S112
$29.75

70S113
$48.00

70S112   70S110

59S66
$29.50

59S67
$26.75

59S65
$24.50

Tailored Details Are Emphasized in Sports Styles

59S65 Two-piece frock of crepe de Chine fashioned on sports lines trimmed with fagotting ; skirt on a bodice top with plaits at sides; plain back; in fern green ; Jenny rose or Copen ; sizes 14, 16, 18 and 20 years . **$24.50**

59S66 Two-piece frock of figured silk damask with bands of self material applied in box-plait effect; facings and pipings of white silk crepe; skirt on bodice top with box-plaits; plain back ; in maize, peach, French blue or all-white; sizes 14, 16, 18 and 20 years . **$29.50**

59S67 One-piece frock of crepe de Chine with contrasting pipings; skirt is box-plaited finished with pockets; in navy, bois de rose or cornflower blue ; sizes 14, 16, 18 and 20 years **$26.75**

56S30
$59.50

56S31
$58.00

56S32
$25.00

56S30　56S31

Spring Suits in Three-piece and Two-piece Styles

56S30　Three-piece tailored costume suit of tweed mixture with overblouse of striped silk shirting; short box-coat; box-plaited at center-back; wrap-around skirt on a bodice top; in blue or gray mixture; sizes 14, 16, 18 and 20 years (for details of blouse see small view)　**$59.50**

56S31　Three-piece tailored costume suit of charmeen with an overblouse of rajah with convertible collar; coat is finished with side-strappings of self-material and buckles over pockets; wrap-around skirt on bodice top; in navy with white blouse or tan with natural blouse; sizes 14, 16 18 and 20 years (for details of blouse see small view)　.　.　.　.　.　.　.　.　.　.　.　.　.　.　**$58.00**

56S31A May be specially ordered in black, with blouse of white rajah　.　.　.　.　.　.　.　.　.　.　.　**$58.00**

56S32　Two-piece sports suit of wool tweed with a single-breasted box coat; two-piece skirt with darts at hips and finished with pocket; in tan or gray mixture; sizes 14, 16, 18 and 20 years (may be specially ordered in sizes 36, 38 and 40 bust)　.　.　.　.　.　.　**$25.00**

42S56A
90¢

38S61
$5.25

38S60
$4.50

42S56
$5.50

42S58
$18.50

42S59
$9.85

42S57
$25.00

38S62
$4.50

42S55
$5.75

42S60
$24.50

The Spring Wardrobe
of the Junior Miss

Scale of sizes for Junior Misses:

Sizes	13	15	17	years
Lengths	41	42	43	inches

42S55 One-piece frock of cotton print with plain collar and cuffs; plaited front and belted back; in lavender-and-green, tan-and-red or blue-and-brown; sizes 13, 15 and 17 years **$5.75**

42S56 Raincoat of rubberized material in bright colors; convertible collar; leather straps; raglan shoulder; in red, green or French blue; sizes 13, 15 and 17 years **$5.50**

42S56A Hat to match No. 42S56 . . . . **$ .90**

42S56B Yellow or green slicker of oilcloth with leather strap at neck; set-in sleeves; sizes 13, 15 and 17 years **$5.00**

42S56C Sou'wester to match slicker 42S56B, in green or yellow **$ .90**

42S57 Well-tailored sports coat of tweed with inverted plaits; silk-lined; in green or tan pin-checked tweed; 13, 15 and 17 years   **$25.00**

42S57A Same style as No. 42S57, in plain navy cheviot   . .**$25.00**

42S58 Practical coat of fancy checked wool plaid, with slot seams; contrasting color insets of flannel; in tan, rose or green, sizes 13, 15 and 17 years **$18.50**

42S58A Same style as No. 42S58 in plain navy cheviot . . **$18.50**

42S59 One-piece tailored frock of mottled wool jersey, trimmed with white flannel; in green, tan or rose; in sizes 13, 15 and 17 years **$9.85**

42S60 Junior misses' two-piece suit of fancy striped tweed, finished with contrasting color flannel; silk lined; in gray or tan tweed; sizes 13, 15 and 17 years **$24.50**

42S60A Same style as No. 42S60; in all-navy twill. . . . **$24.50**

38S60 Felt hat in white, tan or Copen with felt trimming . **$4.50**

38S61 Hat of peanut straw, trimmed with grosgrain ribbon; in white or navy. **$5.25**

38S62 Felt hat in white or henna, with felt trimming . . . **$4.50**

42S70
$7.85

42S71
$16.75

42S73
$9.75

42S72
$12.85

42S76
$16.50

42S75
$22.50

The Needs of
the In≠Between≠Age Are
Carefully Considered

42S70   Frock of rayon with circular skirt is prettily trimmed
with plaid rayon, in peach, blue, or green; sizes 13, 15 and
17 years **$7.85**
42S71   Frock of crepe de Chine with contrasting color
smocking and trimming; in bois de rose, green or navy;
sizes 13, 15 and 17 years **$16.75**
42S72   Sports frock of rainbow-striped silk broadcloth
with convertible collar and plain colored trimming; in blue,
rose or helio predominating; in sizes 13, 15 and 17 years
                                          $12.85

42S73   Flowered cotton crepe finished with contrasting
pipings and trimmings; full gathered skirt; in green, rose or
blue; sizes 13, 15 and 17 years **$9.75**
42S75   Two-piece afternoon frock of georgette with full
circular skirt, and blouse trimmed with flowers; in carmine
red, green or melon rose; sizes 13, 15 and 17 years **$22.50**
42S76   High-necked frock of crepe de Chine with insets of
gold lace; flare skirt; in green, navy, leather, bois de rose;
sizes 13, 15 and 17 years **$16.50**

Women's Hosiery and New Foot Notes

Balta Shoes, exclusive with B. Altman & Co., are shown on fashion pages throughout the book. Prices upon request

Betalph Hosiery is exclusive with B. ALTMAN & CO.

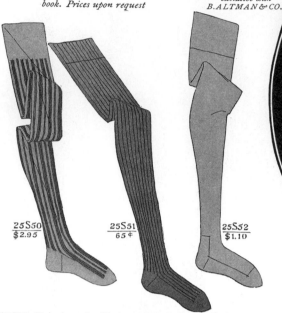

25S50
$2.95

25S51
65¢

25S52
$1.10

25S54
$2.95

53S73
$11.50

25S54 Women's imported novelty lisle sports hose; pattern may vary **$2.95**

For description of No. 53S73, see page 79

25S53 Women's cotton hose; medium weight; full-fashioned; black, white, unbleached, gray or Russia tan; per pair (*not illustrated*) **$1.00**

25S50 Women's novelty ribbed sport hose of silk and lisle mixture, two-toned effect and self-colorings; per pair **$2.95**
25S51 Women's ribbed lisle sport hose; black, white, gray, beige, camel, cordovan; per pair . . . . **$ .65**
25S52 Women's lisle hose; full-fashioned; medium weight; black, white, beige, nude, light gray, dark gray, Russia tan or cordovan; per pair **$1.10**

53S60
$12.75

53S61
$14.00

53S60 A very smart Grecian sandal of black suede with patent leather applique; spike heels; per pair **$12.75**
53S60A Same model as No. 53S60 in parchment kid with Sauterne kid applique; per pair **$12.75**
53S60B Same model as No. 53S60 in tan kid and tan lizard calf applique; per pair . . . **$12.75**

53S61 New pumps of gray kidskin with applique of gray lizard calf; per pair **$14.00**
53S61A Same model as No. 53S61 in parchment kid with applique of Sauterne kid; per pair **$14.00**
53S61B Same model as No. 53S61 in patent leather with applique of tan lizard calf; per pair **$14.00**

53S62
$11.50

53S63
$8.00

53S62 White cloth strap pump with patent leather or with white calfskin applique; per pair **$11.50**
53S62A Same as No. 53S62 in patent leather with black calfskin applique or Ascot tan kid applique; per pair **$12.50**

53S63 Strap pump of tan calfskin with tan lizard calfskin applique; per pair **$8.00**
53S63A Same as No. 53S63 in patent leather with tan lizard calfskin applique; per pair . . **$8.00**

53S64
$8.50

53S65
$8.75

53S64 Patent leather oxford ties with dark tan lizard calfskin applique; per pair . . . **$8.50**
53S64A Same as No. 53S64 in tan calfskin with tan lizard calfskin applique; per pair . . . **$8.50**

53S65 Good looking step-in pumps of dark tan alligator calfskin; per pair **$8.75**
53S65A Same style as No. 53S65 in patent leather; per pair **$8.75**

Unless otherwise specified, Women's Footwear is obtainable in the following sizes: 2½, 3 and 3½ in B, C, and D widths. 4 to 7½ in AA to D widths.

Women's Sports Hose and Footwear

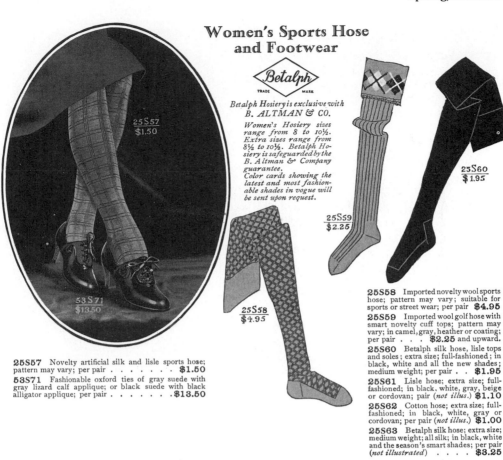

Betalph
TRADE MARK

Betalph Hosiery is exclusive with
B. ALTMAN & CO.
Women's Hosiery sizes range from 8 to 10½. Extra sizes range from 8½ to 10½. Betalph Hosiery is safeguarded by the B. Altman & Company guarantee. Color cards showing the latest and most fashionable shades in vogue will be sent upon request.

25S57
$1.50

53S71
$13.50

25S58
$4.95

25S59
$2.25

25S60
$1.95

25S57 Novelty artificial silk and lisle sports hose; pattern may vary; per pair **$1.50**
53S71 Fashionable oxford ties of gray suede with gray lizard calf applique; or black suede with black alligator applique; per pair **$13.50**

25S58 Imported novelty wool sports hose; pattern may vary; suitable for sports or street wear; per pair **$4.95**
25S59 Imported wool golf hose with smart novelty cuff tops; pattern may vary; in camel, gray, heather or coating; per pair . . . **$2.25** and upward.
25S60 Betalph silk hose, lisle tops and soles; extra size; full-fashioned; in black, white and all the new shades; medium weight; per pair . . **$1.95**
25S61 Lisle hose; extra size; full-fashioned; in black, white, gray, beige or cordovan; pair (*not illus.*) **$1.10**
25S62 Cotton hose; extra size; full-fashioned; in black, white, gray or cordovan; per pair (*not illus.*) **$1.00**
25S63 Betalph silk hose; extra size; medium weight; all silk; in black, white and the season's smart shades; per pair (*not illustrated*) **$3.25**

53S70
$12.00

53S70 Very much in fashion are oxford ties of patent leather with spike heels; per pair . . . **$12.00**
53S70A Same style as No. 53S70; in black ooze with patent leather applique; Ascot tan kid with tan snake calf applique; per pair **$12.00**
53S70B Same as No. 53S70; white kid; pair **$12.00**

53S71
$13.50

53S71A Same style as No. 53S71; in Sauterne kid with tan lizard calf applique; or patent leather with tan snake calf applique **$13.50**
53S71B Same style as No. 53S71; in tan alligator with Sauterne kid applique or black alligator with tan alligator applique **$16.50**

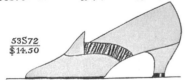

53S72
$14.50

53S72 Attractive pump of white kidskin with black and white lizard calfskin saddle; per pair . **$14.50**
53S72A Same style as No. 53S72; in all white kidskin; per pair **$14.50**

53S73
$11.50

53S73 Sports oxfords of white buckskin with saddles of tan or black alligator calfskin; also black patent leather or white buckskin; imported crepe rubber soles; per pair **$11.50**
53S73A Same style as No. 53S73; in tan Scotch grain calfskin with dark tan saddle or smoke elkskin with dark tan calfskin saddle; per pair . . . **$10.50**

53S74
$3.50

53S74 D'Orsay slippers of quilted satin; in black, old rose or delph blue; sizes 3 to 8; medium widths; no half sizes; per pair **$3.50**

53S75
$2.50

53S75 Boudoir slippers of black leather; sizes 2½ to 8; medium widths; per pair **$2.50**

Unless otherwise stated, Women's Footwear is obtainable in the following sizes: 2½, 3 and 3½ in B, C and D widths; 4 to 7½ in AA to D widths. For Men's Hosiery, see page 56

Frocks for the Little Girl

57S80 One-piece frock of tub silk with collar, cuffs and pipings of white silk; ribbon tie; in white-and-red, rose-and-white or green-and-white predominating; sizes 8 to 16 years . **$9.75**

57S81 Charmingly simple frock of rayon has a narrow belt of self-material across back; collar, cuffs and pipings of white silk broadcloth; peach, blue or green; sizes 6 to 10 years . **$5.95**

57S82 Bloomer frock of cotton print, with white organdie collar, cuffs and ruffling; in blue-and-white, green-and-white, or gold-and-white; sizes 6 to 10 years **$4.75**

57S83 Delightful frock of cotton voile with collar and cuffs of self-material edged with lace; ribbon tie is held in position with hand-embroidery; in peach, light blue or pink; sizes 6 to 10 years **$3.10**

57S84 Practical bloomer frock of plain colored chambray trimmed with touches of embroidery; in blue, green or brown; sizes 6 to 10 years **$2.95**

57S85 Unusually smart one-piece frock of figured sateen, is a long-waisted model with plaited skirt and collar and cuffs of white dimity, finished with hand-stitching; ribbon belt; in blue, rose or green predominating; sizes 8 to 14 years . . . **$4.75**

57S86 Charming bloomer frock of wool challis made with a yoke; collar and cuffs of handkerchief linen finished with hand-embroidered dots; in navy-and-white; green-and-white or red-and-white; sizes 6 to 10 years **$9.85**

57S87 Bloomer frock of tan pongee trimmed with wool embroidery with the collar and cuffs of Copen or red rayon to match embroidery; sizes 6 to 10 years **$5.95**

38S75 Hat of natural leghorn, rolls off the face and is bound and trimmed with black velvet **$4.25**

38S76 Smart hat of Palmetto green or Copen blue faille; sectional crown and leghorn brim **$6.00**

38S77 Tailored hat of natural leghorn, trimmed with black or Copen blue moire ribbon **$9.00**

School and Playtime Frocks

57S95 Serviceable and smart is this two-piece frock consisting of a box-plaited skirt of polka-dotted cotton broadcloth with a blouse of plain broadcloth, buttoning to the skirt; in green or blue; sizes 6 to 16 years **$4.50**

57S96 Checked gingham is employed to fashion this one-piece frock with collar, cuffs and tie of white rep and a touch of hand-stitching trimming the pockets; in green-and-white, blue-and-white or pink-and-white; sizes 8 to 16 years **$2.95**

57S97 A one-piece frock of Devonshire with a two-piece effect has collar, cuffs and belt trimmed with a band of white cotton broadcloth; in peach, blue or green; sizes 8 to 14 years **$2.95**

57S98 Smocked bloomer frock of cotton print is a collarless model, finished with a ribbon; in blue, rose or green on white background, sizes 6 to 10 years. **$4.95**

57S99 Cotton broadcloth dimity in a dainty flowered design fashions this charming bloomer frock with patch pockets; white background with pink or blue predominating; sizes 6 to 10 years **$5.25**

57S100 Cotton print is used to make this bloomer frock with collar and cuffs of handkerchief linen finished with touches of hand-embroidery; in Copen, orchid or red; sizes 6 to 10 years **$4.95**

57S101 Bloomer frock of fine quality chambray with collar, cuffs and trimming of white dimity; in Copen, pink or tan; sizes 6 to 10 years **$3.75**

57S102 A straight-line one-piece frock of striped cotton broadcloth finished with a ribbon tie; in blue-and-white, rose-and-white or green-and-white; sizes 8 to 16 years **$3.90**

57S103 Bloomer dress of chambray with collar, cuffs and trimming of contrasting chambray finished with touches of hand-stitching; in brown, Copen or green; sizes 6 to 10 years **$2.95**

38S92 Natural leghorn hat in poke shape bound and trimmed with black velvet ribbon **$4.25**

57S106
$18.75 (set)

57S107
$13.75 (set)

38S111
$6.75

57S108
$4.95 (set)

57S109
$15.75 (set)

57S110
$22.50

New Coats with Hats to Match

57S106 Novelty checked coating in green-and-white or Copen-and-tan is used for this attractive outfit consisting of a coat in a semi-raglan style and smart hat to match; sizes 6 to 16 years; complete **$18.75**

57S106A Separate coat; sizes 6 to 16 years . .**$15.00**

57S107 Practical outfit consisting of a coat and hat of blue, tan or rust tweed; coat is a double-breasted model with pockets, and is lined with cotton twill; hat is trimmed with leather; sizes 6 to 16 years; outfit complete . . .**$13.75**

57S107A Separate coat, sizes 6 to 16 years . .**$10.50**

57S107B Same model as No. 57S107A, navy cheviot with brass buttons; sizes 6 to 16 years **$13.75**

57S107C Same model as No. 57S107A, tan covert cloth with bone buttons; sizes 6 to 16 years **$15.50**

57S108 Slicker and hat of blue, rose or green rubberized material; raglan model; collar lined with corduroy and finished with a strap; sizes 6 to 16 years, complete . . **$4.95**

57S109 Wool basket-weave material is combined with fancy plaid tweed to fashion this charming coat and hat outfit; coat is single-breasted with slashed pockets; lined with cotton twill; in rust or green; sizes 6 to 16 years .**$15.75**

57S109A Separate coat; sizes 6 to 16 years . .**$12.50**

57S110 A dressy coat of navy or green poiret twill with collar and cuffs of embroidered banding; silk lined throughout; in sizes 6 to 16 years **$22.50**

38S111 Hat of French felt, faced and trimmed with Milan hemp; in white or navy **$6.75**

Riding Habits and Gymnasium Apparel for the Girl

52S110 Children's riding habit (coat and breeches) of tan linen; sizes 8, 10 and 12 years **$14.50**

52S111 Children's riding habit (coat and breeches) of excellent quality tweed; in brown or gray, well-tailored straight-line coat; sizes 8, 10 and 12 years . **$29.50**

52S111A Same model as No. 52S111 may be ordered in sizes 13, 15 and 17 years **$32.50**

57S115 Middy blouse of khaki twill; collar and cuffs trimmed with white braid; sizes 6 to 20 years . **$1.75**

57S115A Same model as No. 57S115 in Copen blue cotton suiting; sizes 6 to 20 years **$1.75**

57S116 Plaited bloomers of khaki twill; sizes 6 to 20 years **$1.85**

57S116A Same model as No. 57S116 in Copen blue cotton suiting; sizes 6 to 20 years **$1.85**

57S117 Middy and bloomer suit of Copen blue cotton suiting; bloomers button to the blouse which is trimmed with white braid; sizes 6 to 12 years **$2.95**

57S118 Middy blouse of white cotton twill, with short sleeves; sizes 6 to 20 years **$1.35**

57S119 Full-plaited bloomers of storm serge for the gymnasium, camp or sports wear; reinforced; in navy, black or brown; sizes 6 to 20 years **$3.85**

52S110 $14.50

52S111 $29.50

57S115 $1.75

57S116 $1.85

57S117 $2.95

57S118 $1.35

57S119 $3.85

Frocks of Practical Fabrics for Wee Girls

49S125 Bloomer frock of Copen or maize handkerchief linen, with hand-embroidery and hemstitching; sizes 2 to 5+ **$5.25**
49S126 Frock of white cotton voile daintily trimmed with hand-stitching in pink; sizes 2 to 4 years **$2.95**
49S127 Bloomer frock of white cotton print, with blue or tan dots; white collar and cuffs; sizes 2 to 5+ **$2.85**
49S128 Frock of printed lawn in blue or peach, trimmed with white frills and hand-stitching; sizes 2 to 5+ **$3.35**
49S129 Bloomer dress of blue or peach cotton print, with white collar; sizes 2 to 5+ **$1.95**
49S130 Bloomer dress of blue or rose-figured cotton broadcloth, with white lawn collar and cuffs; sizes 2 to 5+ **$3.75**
49S131 Bloomer frock of imported blue or rose-figured dimity on white background; sizes 2 to 5+ **$4.50**

49S132 Dress of white lawn with blue or red dots, trimmed with picoted ruffles; sizes 2 and 3 years **$1.50**
49S133 Bloomer frock of cotton print in blue or pink, trimmed with frill and plain color binding; sizes 2 to 5+ **$3.75**
49S134 Dress of white crossbar batiste, trimmed with hand-embroidery; sizes 2 to 5 years **$2.95**
49S135 Bloomer dress of green or maize chambray with white collar; sizes 2 to 5+ **$2.00**
49S136 Bloomer frock of figured rayon with white sateen collar, cuffs and trimming finished with hand-stitching; in white with red design; sizes 2 to 5+ **$5.65**
49S137 Bloomer frock of checked sateen, in rose or green, with collar, cuffs and trimming of white broadcloth, finished with hand-stitching; sizes 2 to 5+ **$4.50**

49S138 Frock of imported voile, in maize or powder blue, trimmed with white collar and cuffs; hand-stitching; sizes 2 to 5+ **$2.95**
49S139 Bloomer dress of helio or peach imported chambray, with white trimming; hand-smocked; sizes 2 to 5+ **$4.10**
49S140 Bloomer dress of peach, or helio cotton broadcloth, trimmed with white broadcloth and hand-stitching; sizes 2 to 5 years **$2.95**
49S141 White velvet bear; cuddle toy **$1.50**
49S142 Bedtime kitten pillow . . . . **$ .55**
49S143 Stockinet doll **$1.10**
49S144 Patty-cake doll dressed in gingham **$1.50**
49S145 Terry cloth dog; with voice **$1.45**

5+ is an intermediate size, larger than size 5, and smaller than the regular 6

Play and Dress-up Togs for Little Boys

49S100 Boys' suit with blouse of white linene, and trousers of blue or light brown peggy cloth; sizes 2 to 5 years **$1.10**
49S100A Same as 49S100, all white cotton broadcloth; 2 to 5 yrs. **$2.90**
49S101 Boys' suit with blouse of oyster white linen finished with hand-stitching and trimmed to match the trousers of blue or lavender linen ; sizes 2 to 5 years **$5.25**
49S102 Boys' regulation suit of Devonshire cloth; in all-Copen or white with blue collar; sizes 2 to 5 years **$3.75**
49S103 Boys' suit of light brown or blue peggy cloth, with white pique collar and hand-stitching; sizes 2 to 5 years **$2.10**
49S104 Boys' suit with white checked cotton blouse and trousers of blue or light brown peggy cloth;   sizes 2 to 5 years **$2.25**
49S105 Boys' suit of blue or green peggy cloth with hand-smocking; sizes 2 to 5 years **$2.25**

49S113 Boys' suit with smocked blouse of white dimity; trimmed with collar and cuffs of green or maize Devonshire cloth, to match the trousers; sizes 2 to 5 years . . . **$2.95**
49S114 Bear, brown plush, on wheels **$1.45**
49S115 Cat of gray plush . . . **$1.45**
49S116 Rubber horn . . . . **$ .50**
50S130 Romper of chambray trimmed with hand-embroidery on pocket, collar and cuffs of white cotton broadcloth; on-and-off model; in Copen, green, maize or all-white; sizes 1, 2 and 3 years **$1.85**
50S131 Romper of white crossbar dimity; creeper model, sleeveless, square neck; daintily trimmed with picoted frills; 1, 2 and 3 yrs. **$1.25**
50S132 Romper of chambray, opening at side; creeper model trimmed with juvenile braid; in Copen or pink; sizes 1, 2 and 3 years **$1.25**
50S133 Romper of chambray (boys' model) trimmed with white madras collar; in cadet blue, tan or all khaki; sizes 3, 4 and 6 years **$1.45**

49S106 Boys' suit of blue or oyster white linen with white frills and hand smocking; sizes 2 to 4 years **$5.65**
49S107 Boys' suit with white cotton broadcloth blouse and trousers of blue or light brown linen; sizes 2 to 5 years **$4.50**
49S108 Boys' suit of lavender or maize Devonshire cloth with frills of white batiste; sizes 2 to 4 years **$3.75**
49S109 Boys' suit of khaki color jean; sizes 2 to 5 years . . . **$1.75**
49S109A Same as No. 49S109 in blue or tan linen; 2 to 5 years **$2.25**
49S110 Boys' suit of medium blue or light brown peggy cloth with white collar and cuffs; sizes 2 to 5 years **$1.10**
49S111 Boys' suit with blouse of white striped dimity with trousers of blue or maize Devonshire cloth; sizes 2 to 4 years **$3.75**
49S112 Boys' suit of blue or green peggy cloth with white linene collar and cuffs; sizes 2 to 5 years **$2.25**
49S112A Boys' suit similar to No. 49S112 in Oliver Twist style, in blue or green peggy cloth; sizes 2 to 5 years **$2.25**

A Litheness Emanates from Gracious Frocks

Just the correct amount of fulness in just the correct place makes a dress becoming to the figure. These two frocks are examples of good distribution of material.

34W45 La France rose with bud and leaves; white, maize, pink or peach, $2.25.

34W46 Pond lily in white, pink or maize, $2.25.

34W47 Corsage of violets in white, purple or mauve, $1.50.

70W39
$39.75

34W45
$2.25

34W46
$2.25

34W47
$1.50

70W40
$37.50

70W39 In this frock of Canton crepe the acme of style perfection is reached. It is dressy without being over-done, smart but not bizarre and the type that is suitable for all occasions. The Jenny collar of fine cream lace and tucked georgette softens the V-neckline. Cuffs to match trim the sleeves. The low waistline is encircled with a band of shirring finished with a metal buckle. The fulness of the tunic is massed at front. Navy, black or beige. Sizes, 34 to 42, $39.75.

70W40 The V-shaped yoke and the trimming on the sleeves of the frock of georgette over crepe de Chine are developed in a harmonizing tone, grey with lighter grey, beige with light tan or navy with flesh. Beaded embroidery is novel and effective. A rhinestone-studded buckle secures the girdle, which is draped over finely plaited panels. Sizes, 34 to 42, $37.50.

Unless otherwise specified, the Women's Dresses illustrated are supplied as follows:

| Bust . . . . | 34 | 36 | 38 | 40 | 42 | 44 inches |
| Entire length of dress, taken from the center back of neck-line to hem of skirt . . . | 45 | 45 | 46 | 47 | 47 | 48 inches |

Where size 46 inches bust may be specially ordered, the length of dress, taken from the center back of neck-line to hem of skirt, will be 49 inches

These Dresses Give a Well-Dressed Look

You know the feeling your favourite dress gives you. Invariably you look your best in it. But that frock will wear out. Let one of these replace it.

15W25 Rhinestones rim this buckle which may be procured with jade, coral or blue galalith center. Size, 2 x 2½ inches, $4.00.

15W26 This motif of silver tinsel twinkles with rhinestones and makes an effective ornament. Size, 7¾ x 3 inches, $6.00. Smaller sizes, $2.25 and $3.00 each.

18W33 This gold-filled slave bracelet is one of the new wide styles so much in demand. $7.50.

70W53
$25.00

18W33
$7.50

15W25
$4.00

15W26
$6.00

70W52
$52.50

70W52 The georgette afternoon frock in naida green with darker green, pinkish beige with cinnamon or queen blue with darker blue is embellished with self-tone embroidery. The apron overskirt is divided in the center to correspond with the vertical line of waist. Fulness gathered to the front is surmounted by an attractive buckle which serves as a finishing note for the crushed girdle. Bands of contrasting colour at the underarms give a slender line. Crepe de Chine foundation. Sizes, 34 to 42, $52.50.

70W53 A dress that should occupy a place in every woman's wardrobe is pictured here. The material is georgette, posed over a crepe de Chine slip. The tiered front crosses over in surplus manner clasping with a metal ornament. The vestee and cuffs in a harmonizing colour are also tucked. Plain straight back navy with tan, hydrangea blue with grey. It can also be procured in all grey or all beige; or specially ordered in all black. Sizes, 34 to 44; size 46 may be specially ordered. $25.00.

59W40 With the front of skirt plaited finely and the neckline exhibiting the fashionable V-shape accentuated by tucking, no wonder this frock is acclaimed one of the season's successes—for these are the points Paris considers essential to chic. It is a copy of Champcommunal, a new couturier. The waistline is indicated by a band of material to which the waist and skirt are joined. The material is flat crepe. Fallow tan, Palmetto green or Chanel blue are the colours. Sizes, 14 to 20, $35.00.

59W41 Lines that produce geometric effects play the stellar rôle in present-day fashions. This vogue is presented in this frock of wool crepe, which is superbly simple and fashioned in a youthful manner. The V-shaped neckline is emphasized by the tucked band which becomes a smart bow tie. In front, the dress is plaited, but in back it is plain. A belt of leather is not to be overlooked. Colours: beige, gooseberry-green or bluebird. Sizes, 14 to 20, $25.00.

59W42 Nothing is newer—or more expressive of youth—than this two-piece daytime dress of flat crepe. The two-tone combination, which it exploits so effectively, is unusual and in the following colours: Madonna blue blouse and Chanel blue skirt or desert tan blouse and oak-brown skirt. Fan-shaped plaited inserts add fulness and smartness to the skirt, which is mounted on a silk bodice. A rippling jabot and plaitings at the collar and sleeves are points of interest. Sizes, 14 to 20 years, $32.50.

19W38 The latest creation of D'Orsay of Paris is "Le Dandy," an exotic new perfume contained in a most attractive black diamond-cut bottle in the following sizes, one ounce, $7.50; two ounces, $13.50 and four ounces, $25.00.

59W41
$25.00

59W40
$35.00

59W42
$32.50

19W38
$7.50

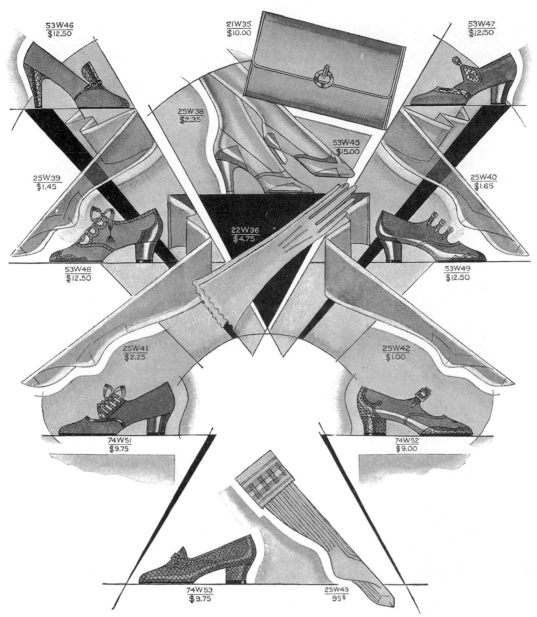

53W46
$12.50

21W35
$10.00

53W47
$12.50

25W38
$2.35

53W45
$15.00

25W39
$1.45

25W40
$1.65

22W36
$4.75

53W48
$12.50

53W49
$12.50

25W41
$2.25

25W42
$1.00

74W51
$9.75

74W52
$9.00

74W53
$9.75

25W43
95¢

In Paris the smartest accessories are beige—and especially chic are the costumes where the accessories—bags, shoes, gloves, etc., form an ensemble of blending beige tones. On this page you will find an ensemble such as we describe, consisting of a suede bag No. 21W35, two-tone slippers of beige kidskin No. 53W45, sheer hose No. 25W38 and pull-on gloves of washable suede, No. 22W36.

21W35 An envelope purse of beige suede to harmonize with shoes and gloves is nicely lined, fitted with purse and mirror. The unique ring clasp is secured with a jewelled marcassite band, $10.00.

22W36 Pull-on beige glove of washable suede to harmonize with bag and shoes; pair, $4.75..

25W38 Women's Betalph chiffon weight silk hose in harmonizing beige tones; pair, $2.35.

53W45 Chaussure Balta step-in pump of two-tone beige kidskin, $15.00. (Made in Paris, exclusively for B. Altman & Co.)

25W39 Full-fashioned medium weight silk hose with lisle tops and soles. Black, white, moonlight, squirrel, gun metal, blue fox, blondine, light blond, almond, alesan, malacca, autumn beige or sand; pair, $1.45.

25W40 Chiffon-weight silk hose in vision, blondine, moonlight, squirrel stone grey, gun metal, blue fox, flesh nude, tanaura, fauvette, alesan, muscade, black or white; pair, $1.65.

25W41 Full-fashioned silk-and-wool hose in camel, neutral grey, dark grey, beaver, pongee, maple, brown, flesh, black or white; pair, $2.25.

25W42 Women's lisle thread hose in sandalwood-brown, beige or grey tones, $1.00.

25W43 Children's wool golf hose with novelty cuffed tops in heather, lovat or oxford. Sizes, 7 to 10½; pair, 95c.

74W51 Young women's oxford of marsela brown suede with applique of brown lizard calfskin; black suede with applique of patent leather or patent leather with applique of black lizard calf, $9.75.

74W52 Young women's strap pump of tan calfskin with tip and back forking of tan grained calfskin, low heel. Sizes 2½ to 8, $9.00.

74W53 Young women's smart step-in pump of tan lizard calfskin with tongue and small buckle in front and low heel. Sizes, 2½ to 8, $9.75.

53W46 The nut brown alligator calfskin underlay is most effective in this pump of brown suede. It also comes in black ooze with an underlay of black lizard calfskin, $12.50.

53W47 Since three leathers are three times as smart as one this strap pump adopts the combination of brown suede with stroller tan kidskin and plaid calfskin; or if one prefers, it can be selected in cherry patent leather with tan kid and plaid calfskin or black patent leather with grey kid and grey plaid calfskin; pair, $12.50.

53W48 This trim oxford comes in black suede with black lizard calfskin trimming; black patent leather with black lizard calfskin trimming or stroller tan kidskin trimmed with cherry patent leather; pair, $12.50.

53W49 A chic, yet practical walking pump which has three straps across instep may be secured in stroller tan kidskin with applique of cherry patent leather; black patent leather with applique of black lizard calfskin; black mat kid with applique of patent leather or black suede with applique of black patent leather; pair, $12.50.

Sizes 2½ to 9 in B and C widths; or 5 to 9 in A A A to C widths.
Young women's shoes are in sizes 2½ to 8 in B, C and D widths. Sizes 4 to 8 in A A to D widths.
Women's hosiery sizes range from 8 to 10½. Extra sizes range from 8½ to 10½.

Betalph
TRADE   MARK

Hosiery is exclusive with B. Altman & Co.

When Sheer Frocks Prevail, Slips Assume Importance

51W38 Just the thing to wear under a filmy chiffon dance frock—a costume slip of georgette crepe, studded with rhinestones. The uneven edge, too, is a pleasing feature : each stone is securely fastened. White, flesh, peach, sweet pea or black. Sizes, 34 to 40, $8.75.

51W39 This costume slip of tub silk in flesh, tan, white or black, boasts a hemstitched top and shadow-proof hem. Sizes, 36 to 44, $2.95

51W40 Tailored costume slip of high lustre rayon, in black, beige, silver, gold or green, is a straight-line model. Sizes, 34 to 44, $4.50.

51W41 Straight-line costume slip of crepe de Chine finished with embroidery and real filet lace has shadow-proof hem and may be selected in white, flesh or tan. Sizes, 34 to 44, $7.95.

51W42 Petticoat of heavy quality crepe de Chine with flounce. Lengths, 26, 28, 30 inches; actual hip size 50 inches, waist 30 inches on elastic. Black, green, beige, old blue or white, $4.25.

47W35 Hand-embroidered Porto Rican nightrobe of white nainsook finished with filet lace edge. Sizes, 15, 16, 17, $2.95.

47W36 Costume slip of sateen (cotton) with decorative hemstitched band at top. The colours are flesh, black, tan, white or navy. Sizes, 36 to 44, $1.95. 47W36A Same model in size 46, $2.50.

79W43 Crepe de Chine vest chemise tailored model, hemstitched band at top finished with real filet edge. Flesh only. Sizes, 34 to 44, $3.95.

Innovations Delight Those of Individual Tastes

51W44 Costume slip of heavy quality radium silk is trimmed with hemstitching and real filet edging at top; shadow-proof hem; plait at back. Colours are flesh or white. Sizes, 34 to 44, $5.75.

51W45 An effective costume slip of crepe de Chine, is daintily adorned with Alencon lace and net with ribbon shoulder straps. Colours: Nile, tea rose, or sweet pea. Sizes, 34 to 44, $6.90.

The following Nos. 47 W38, 47 W39, 47 W40, 47 W41, comprise a set of matching pieces.

47W38 Vest chemise of printed batiste is a tailored model, bound with plain material to harmonize with colour of print. Orchid, red or green designs on white background. Sizes, 36 to 40 inches, $1.50.

47W39 Step-in drawer. of printed batiste to match, with yoke effect at front and elastic at back. Lengths 19, 21, 23 inches, $1.95.

47W40 This nightrobe of printed batiste is a tailored model to match. Sizes, 14 to 17, $2.95.

47W41 Step-in chemise of printed batiste to match above. Sizes, 36 to 40, $1.95.

47W42 Nightrobe of Celanese ninon, an exquisite new material, delightfully soft and lustrous. The sun or frequent tubbing will not affect the colour or the sheen. You may have it in Nile or flesh, daintily trimmed with fancy net. Sizes, 14 to 17, $7.90.

47W43 Chemise of Celanese ninon, matches nightrobe No. 47W42. Sizes, 36 to 40, $5.50.

51W44 $5.75

51W45 $6.90

47W40 $2.95

47W41 $1.95

47W38 $1.50

47W39 $1.95

47W42 $7.90

47W43 $5.50

63M61
$29.00

67M67
$55.00

63M62
$42.00

New Wraps Endorse Slender Lines

63M61 Reversible coat of kashmir and faille, copied from an Aviotty model is so well tailored it can be worn on either the cloth or the silk side with equal success. The coat which is shown worn on the silk side has the same details that encircle the hipline, forming two slashed pockets at each side of the front, repeated on the inside. Black faille lined with natural, green, medium tan or grey kashmir. Sizes, 14, 16, 18 and 20, $29.00. 63M61A Same model may be specially ordered in all-black with black kashmir lining, $29.00.
67M61 Same model in sizes 36 to 46, $29.00.
63M62 Tucks and bows are at present fashion's favourite media for achieving smartness. This coat of fine wool twill adopts both of these advantageously. The bow at the shoulder is of satin. Dyed squirrel at the collar is becoming. Tucks appear at the sides and on the sleeves. The coat is silk lined throughout. Navy, tan or black with cocoa-dyed squirrel. Sizes, 14, 16, 18 and 20, $42.00.
67M62 Same model in sizes 36 to 46, $42.00.
67M67 The panel treatment at the back of this coat is in line with the mode's insistence in maintaining the straightest silhouette possible. The coat is made of black satin lined with crepe de Chine and collared with ermine. The latter may be white or dyed cocoa shade as desired. Either lends a flattering effect. Sizes, 36 to 46, $55.00.
63M67 Same model in sizes 14, 16, 18 and 20, $55.00.

Scale of sizes of Misses' Coats

Sizes:	14	16	18	20	years
Lengths:	41	42	43	44	inches

Flannel Coats are one inch shorter

63M61

67M67

Coats of Slender Lines
Herald Approach
of New Season

34W42
$10.50

34W42 This smart hat of Bangkok
turned up at back with grosgrain binding and motif at side tops the all-white
costume with chic. Besides all-white,
it may be obtained in black or beige,
$10 50.

63W35
$42.00

67W36
$69.00

63W35 Since so many of the new coats are
seamed at the back to give interest, this all-
white coat employs a single slot seam at center
back for this same purpose. The material is
fancy white cheviot and the collar is fluffy white
hare. Well-tailored and exceedingly smart, it is
obtainable in white only and may be worn with
or without belt. Sizes, 14 to 20, $42.00. Size,
14; length, 41 inches; size, 16; length, 42 inches;
size, 18; length, 43 inches; size, 20; length,
44 inches.
67W35 Same model in sizes 36 to 46, $42.00.
Size, 36; length, 45 inches; sizes, 38 to 42; length,
46 inches; sizes, 44-46; length, 47 inches.
67W36 Destined to be one of the season's successes is this new coat, a copy of Patou devel-

oped in a new material, called "Kashedda."
The three stitched inverted plaits at back immedi-
ately identify it with the deft touch of Jean
Patou. Ombre lapin fur, quite the smartest pelt
of the moment, develops the Tuxedo shawl
collar. Lined throughout with crepe de Chine.
White or natural colour Kashedda, or if you prefer,
it may be had in black Kashmir. Sizes, 36 to 44,
$69.00. Size, 36; length, 46 inches; sizes, 38, 40
and 42; length, 47 inches; size, 44; length, 48
inches.

63W36 Same model in sizes 14 to 20, $69.00.
Size, 14; length, 42 inches; size, 16; length, 43
inches; size, 18; length, 44 inches; size, 20;
length, 45 inches.

A fur coat from Altman's is a wise and safe investment,
which returns a high percentage of interest in the comfort which it gives. Unusual values in furs are offered at
this time of year. Prices and descriptions of our large
collection of pelts will be furnished upon request.

Wear These with Assurance

54W32   Novelty tucking is the keynote to smartness in this serviceable overblouse developed in white English broadcloth and moderately priced. Sizes, 34 to 44, $1.95. *For illustration of this blouse showing collar buttoned to neck, see page 18.*

54W40   Three blending tones of rose colour or three shades of green may be chosen for the washable crepe trimming used for this fascinating hand-made dress-length tunic of natural colour silk pongee. It is further adorned with drawn-work and tucks. Long sleeves are trimmed to match front. Collar can be worn closed or in V style. Sizes, 34 to 42, $6.50.

54W41   Reproduced from a Paris model is this decidedly modish dress-length tunic of crepe de Chine, smartly fashioned on ultra chic lines with V neck finished with a tie. Fan plaits and tucks in front of skirt. Colours: Palmetto green, goya red or marron glace (rich tan). Sizes, 14, 16, 18; also 38 and 40, $15.00.

54W36   The popular Vionnet neckline distinguishes this crepe de Chine overblouse with self-toned flower and tucking which are most effectively employed as the trimming. Colours: white, green, slate blue or new shade of rose tan. Sizes, 34 to 42, $7.90.

54W37   Youthful and becoming is this all-white English broadcloth overblouse which introduces scallops and pearl buttons to advantage. Sizes, 34 to 42, $1.95.

54W38   Entirely hand-made is this charming overblouse of natural colour silk pongee with hand-drawn work and embroidered dots in brown. The collar may be worn high or low. Sizes, 34 to 42, $3.75.

54W39   A well-tailored blouse of white English broadcloth such as we have sketched is always practical and always smart. Trim pockets add to its charm. Sizes, 34 to 42, $2.95.

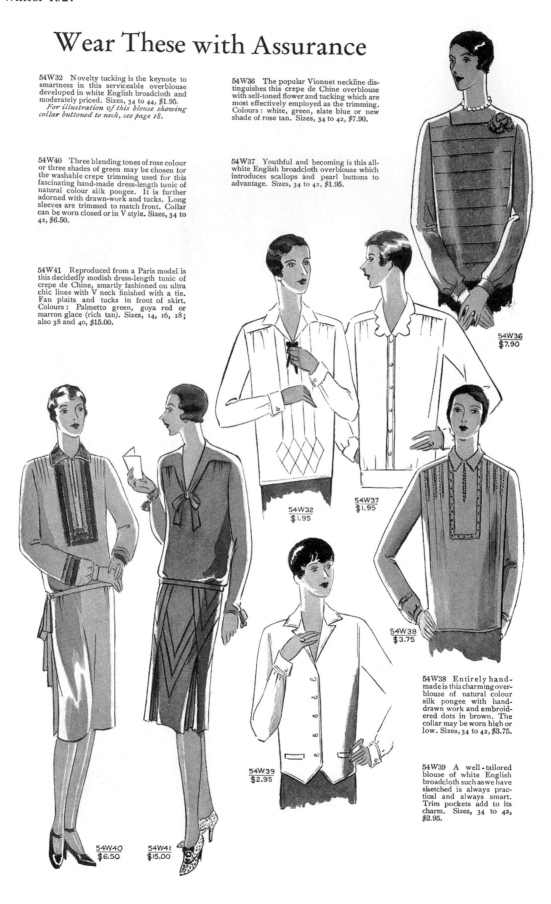

54W36
$7.90

54W32
$1.95

54W37
$1.95

54W38
$3.75

54W39
$2.95

54W40
$6.50

54W41
$15.00

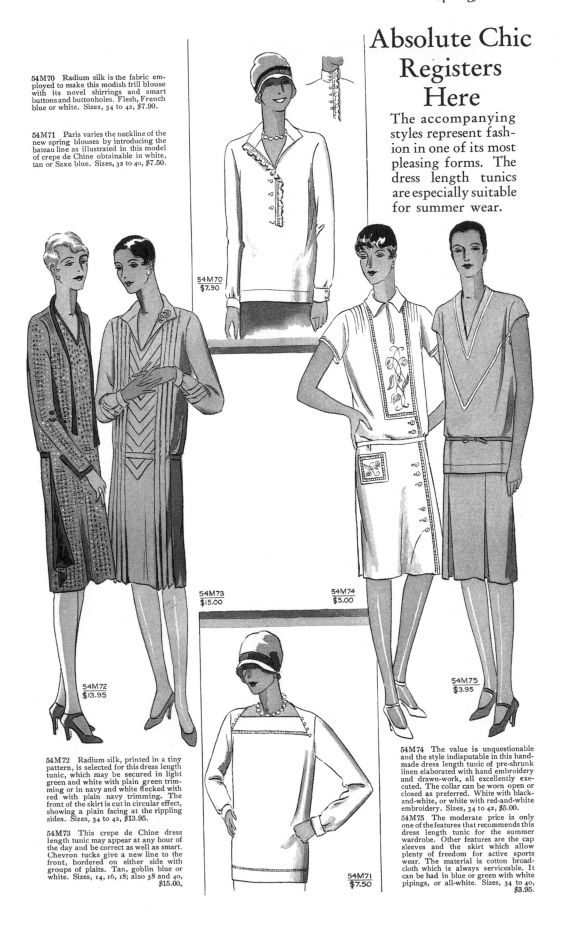

54M70 Radium silk is the fabric employed to make this modish frill blouse with its novel shirrings and smart buttons and buttonholes. Flesh, French blue or white. Sizes, 34 to 42, $7.90.

54M71 Paris varies the neckline of the new spring blouses by introducing the bateau line as illustrated in this model of crepe de Chine obtainable in white, tan or Saxe blue. Sizes, 32 to 40, $7.50.

Absolute Chic Registers Here

The accompanying styles represent fashion in one of its most pleasing forms. The dress length tunics are especially suitable for summer wear.

54M70
$7.90

54M73
$15.00

54M74
$5.00

54M72
$13.95

54M75
$3.95

54M71
$7.50

54M72 Radium silk, printed in a tiny pattern, is selected for this dress length tunic, which may be secured in light green and white with plain green trimming or in navy and white flecked with red with plain navy trimming. The front of the skirt is cut in circular effect, showing a plain facing at the rippling sides. Sizes, 34 to 42, $13.95.

54M73 This crepe de Chine dress length tunic may appear at any hour of the day and be correct as well as smart. Chevron tucks give a new line to the front, bordered on either side with groups of plaits. Tan, goblin blue or white. Sizes, 14, 16, 18; also 38 and 40, $15.00.

54M74 The value is unquestionable and the style indisputable in this hand-made dress length tunic of pre-shrunk linen elaborated with hand embroidery and drawn-work, all excellently executed. The collar can be worn open or closed as preferred. White with black-and-white, or white with red-and-white embroidery. Sizes, 34 to 42, $5.00.

54M75 The moderate price is only one of the features that recommends this dress length tunic for the summer wardrobe. Other features are the cap sleeves and the skirt which allow plenty of freedom for active sports wear. The material is cotton broadcloth which is always serviceable. It can be had in blue or green with white pipings, or all-white. Sizes, 34 to 40, $3.95.

Rare Combinations of Beauty and Service

47W47 This nightrobe of white nainsook is a tailored model with kimono sleeves. Sizes, 14 to 17, 95c. 47W47A Same style in cambric. Sizes, 14 to 17, 95c.

47W48 A most attractive nightrobe of silk sheen (cotton) in flesh, Nile or sweet-pea, has a round neck finished with crochet lace and filet lace edging. Sizes, 14 to 16, $2.95.

47W49 Athletic combination of cotton material. In white or flesh. Sizes, 36 to 44, $1.00. 47W49A Same model with closed crotch. Sizes, 36 to 44, $1.25.

47W50 Hand-embroidered Porto Rican nightrobe of nainsook with edge of Val. lace. The dainty colours are flesh, honey, white or orchid. Sizes, 15 to 17, $1.50.

Scale of sizes of Nightrobes

Sizes	14	15	16	17	18
Bust	36	38	40	42	44 and 46

47W47	47W48	47W49
95¢	$2.95	$1.00

47W51 Nightrobe of white cambric with tucked yoke and filet lace insertion prettily finished at neck and sleeves with hemstitched ruffle, edged with filet. Sizes, 14 to 17, $1.95.

47W52 Costume slip of cotton-and-rayon in flesh or white, with cream lace effectively used to trim the top and bottom. Matches nightrobe No. 47W63 and dance set No. 47W60 shown on page 29. Sizes, 36 to 40, $2.95.

47W53 Gayly printed cotton with the aid of white trimming bands makes this attractive two-piece slip-over pyjama where blue, tan or orchid may be the predominating shades. Sizes, 36 to 40, $1.75.

47W54 Dainty step-in chemise of voile with fine plaitings and cream lace bands matches nightrobe No. 47W62, shown on page 29. Honeydew, orchid, flesh or rose. Sizes, 36 to 40, $2.95.

47W52
$2.95

47W50	47W51	47W53
$1.50	$1.95	$1.75

47W54
$2.95

Easy to Tub, and
Easy to Wear

47W57 Porto Rican costume slip of white nainsook with hand-embroidery and drawn-work has picot lace edge at top and deep hem. Sizes, 36 to 44, $1.85.

47W58 Bloomers of novelty cotton-and-rayon material. Flesh or white. Lengths, 19 and 21 inches, $1.50. **47W58A** Bloomers of striped dimity. White or flesh. Lengths, 25 and 27 in., 95c. (*Not illustrated.*)

47W59 Quite remarkable value is presented in this Porto Rican step-in chemise of white or pink nainsook with hemstitching and touches of hand-embroidery. Sizes, 36 to 44, $1.00.

47W60 Cream lace shows to advantage in the dance set of cotton-and-rayon to match gown No. 47W63 and costume slip No. 47W52 (on page 28). The bandeau is well-made and is obtainable in sizes 32 to 36. The bloomers are especially designed for dancing. Lengths, 19 and 21 inches. Flesh or Nile, $3.50.

47W61 Nightrobe of white cambric with V neck finished with tucking and featherstitching and narrow edge of embroidery. Sizes, 14 to 17, $1.95.

47W57
$1.85

47W58
$1.50

47W59
$1.00

47W62 This charming nightrobe is of cotton voile richly trimmed with Valenciennes lace. Matches chemise No. 47W54 shown on page 28. Flesh, orchid, rose or honeydew. Sizes, 14 to 17, $1.95.

47W63 Nightrobe made of dainty cotton-and-rayon fabric, is a pretty model with cream lace and rosebuds. Matches dance set No. 47W60 and costume slip No. 47W52 (on page 28). May be had in flesh or Nile. Sizes, 14 to 17, $3.65.

47W64 Cunning two-piece slip-over pyjamas of cotton crepe shows a figured crepe jumper in variegated colours with white trimming bands and white trousers with figured bands. Sizes, 36 to 40, $1.95.

47W61
$1.95

47W62
$1.95

47W63
$3.65

47W64
$1.95

47W60
$3.50 Set.

45M70
$1.50

47M128
$1.00

47M131
$1.50

47M132
$1.95

47M133
$5.75

47M129
$1.95

47M130
$1.65

45M70 This bandeau of cream lace lined with net and finished with ribbon shoulder straps fastens with hooks and eyes at the back. Sizes, 32 to 38, $1.50.

47M128 Athletic combination of light weight cotton material in white or pink. Sizes, 36 to 44, $1.00 or size 46, $1.25. **47M128A** Same model with closed crotch. Sizes, 36 to 44, $1.25.

47M129 Attractive two-piece slip-over pajamas of novelty striped cotton material in effective rainbow colourings. Lavender, blue, green or tan predominating. Sizes, 36 to 40, $1.95.

47M130 Hand-embroidered Porto Rican costume slip of white nainsook with deep hem and inverted plait at either side. Sizes, 36 to 44, $1.65. **47M130A** Similar model of rayon with tailored hem at top; has inverted plait at sides and deep hem. Colours: white, flesh, tan or black. Sizes, 36 to 44, $1.65.

47M131 Hand-embroidered Porto Rican step-in chemise of white nainsook finished with an edge of filet lace. Sizes, 36 to 44, $1.50.

47M132 Two-piece slip-over pajamas of cotton crepe in blue, pink or lavender trimmed with band of figured crepe. Sizes, 36 to 40, $1.95.

47M133 Celanese satin in soft shades to harmonize with sheer frocks makes lustrous costume slip in straight line effect with cream lace bordering the top. In pink, white, black or Sahara tan. Sizes, 36 to 44, $5.75.

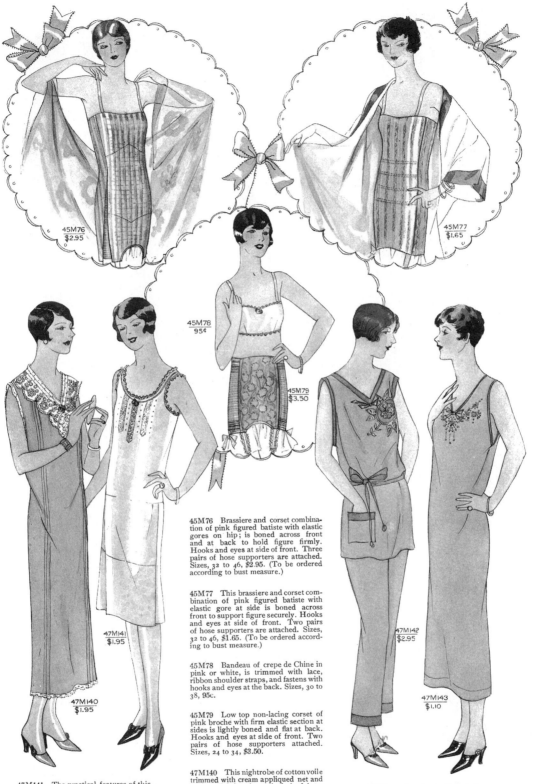

45M76
$2.95

45M77
$1.65

45M78
95¢

45M79
$3.50

47M141
$1.95

47M140
$1.95

47M142
$2.95

47M143
$1.10

45M76 Brassiere and corset combination of pink figured batiste with elastic gores on hip; is boned across front and at back to hold figure firmly. Hooks and eyes at side of front. Three pairs of hose supporters are attached. Sizes, 32 to 46, $2.95. (To be ordered according to bust measure.)

45M77 This brassiere and corset combination of pink figured batiste with elastic gore at side is boned across front to support figure securely. Hooks and eyes at side of front. Two pairs of hose supporters are attached. Sizes, 32 to 46, $1.65. (To be ordered according to bust measure.)

45M78 Bandeau of crepe de Chine in pink or white, is trimmed with lace, ribbon shoulder straps, and fastens with hooks and eyes at the back. Sizes, 30 to 38, 95c.

45M79 Low top non-lacing corset of pink broche with firm elastic section at sides is lightly boned and flat at back. Hooks and eyes at side of front. Two pairs of hose supporters attached. Sizes, 24 to 34, $3.50.

47M140 This nightrobe of cotton voile trimmed with cream appliqued net and narrow Val. lace is particularly dainty; in pink, nile or helio. Sizes, 14 to 17, $1.95.

47M142 Delightful for warm weather are these two-piece pajamas of coloured cotton voile with touches of embroidery and bands of contrasting colour. In peach, flesh or nile. Sizes, 36 to 40, $2 95.

47M141 The practical features of this white nainsook costume slip are the built-up shoulders, plaits at sides and deep hem. The trimming consists of filet lace insertion, French knots and narrow filet edge around neck and armholes. Sizes, 36 to 44, $1.95. **47M141A** Similar style of rayon with built-up shoulders and inverted plaits. Colours: white, flesh, tan or black. Sizes, 36 to 44, $2.95.

47M143 A hand-embroidered Porto Rican nightrobe of pink or white nainsook; may be selected with a round or V-neckline finished with coloured binding. Assorted designs. Sizes, 15, 16, 17, $1.10.

59M83	59M84	34M107	59M85	59M86
$19.50	$22.50	$11.25 (Hat)	$29.00	$19.50

Paris Inspired These Misses' Frocks

59M83 This one-piece frock of georgette is made with a series of tucks at the waistline to simulate the favoured two-piece mode. The sleeves are also finished with tucks and are augmented with tiny buttons and contrasting band trimming in the same manner as the front jabot collar. The skirt is plaited across the front and the back is plain. May be chosen in navy with white, green with tan or all-white. Sizes, 14, 16, 18 and 20, $19.50.

59M84 A jabot-trimmed two-piece frock of crepe de Chine that carries out the two-tone theme to perfection sponsors the lighter shade for the blouse which is made rather long in order that one may adjust it in the approved manner. The contrasting skirt on a silk bodice top is plaited in front as are so many smart skirts. The effective combinations in which this dress may be selected are yellow-and-black, white-and-black or salmon-and-black. Sizes, 14, 16, 18 and 20, $22.50.

59M85 An intricate wrap-around skirt—unusually plaited details and a wide girdle of the material unite, in this afternoon frock of flat crepe, to make it delightfully individual. The skirt slashed at the back is piped in the same contrasting shade as that used for the youthful collar finished with the inevitable bow. The colours are navy with Copen trimming, light green with darker green or black with white. Sizes, 14, 16, 18 and 20, $29.00.

59M86 Arrestingly youthful in style is this two-piece frock which will meet the immediate approval of any young girl. The blouse of flat silk crepe has invisible tucks all around the bottom to make it fit snugly about the hips. The skirt of printed silk crepe mounted on a bodice top gains fulness with inverted plaits in front. In white-and-navy or white-and-black. Sizes, 14, 16, 18 and 20, $19.50.

34M107 Homespun felt is used for this good-looking hat. It is trimmed with two shades of grosgrain ribbon around the crown and the brim turns up at front. Colours: green or grey, $11.25.

34M106
$15.00(Hat)

34M108
$6.00(Hat)

70M95
$22.50

70M96
$25.00

70M97
$19.75

For the Woman Who Knows Good Style

70M95   Washable crepe de Chine in white, orchid or green is the fabric used for this dress where stress is placed upon straight lines by the panels of tucking alternating with box plaits. Tucks also appear at the back and at cuffs and pockets. Sizes, 34 to 44, $22.50.

34M106   For description of hat No. 34M106, see page 11.

70M96   This very useful frock of dotted silk crepe has a panel treatment down the front which produces a coat effect, a line that is much in favour at the present time. Folds forming tiers are placed at the side fronts. A frilled vestee of plain white georgette with cuffs to match completes the attractive whole. The dress comes in two colours, navy dots on white ground or white dots on black ground. Sizes, 34 to 44, $25.00.

34M108   The felt hat pictured has a medium size brim and grosgrain ribbon treatment around the crown. The colours offered are grey or beige, $6.00.

70M97   This debonair two-piece frock of tub silk has more than one feature to recommend it from a fashion standpoint. It presents unquestionable taste and smart style. The surplice closing of the front tying in a bow at the side produces a line that is becoming to all. So chic is the frock within itself that trimming is completely eliminated. The skirt, on a bodice top, laps to the side to correspond with the fashioning of the blouse. White, orchid or apricot are the colours offered. Sizes, 34 to 44, $19.75.

Scale of sizes of Women's Dresses. Unless otherwise specified, the Women's Dresses illustrated are supplied as follows:

Size:	34	36	38	40	42	44	46
Entire length of dress, taken from the center back of neckline to hem of skirt. Lengths:	43	44	45	45	46	46	47

38M75	42M60	34M103	42M61	42M62	42M63
$6.00 (Hat)	$5.75	$3.75(Hat)	$16.50	$16.50	$12.75

Young Girls Confer Particular Charm
on Summer Frocks

42M60 Here is a typical junior misses' summer-time frock of patterned cotton voile in a style that is very attractive. Plain colour contrasting voile trimming appears at the becoming neckline and bottom of skirt which is shirred at the low waistline. The back is plain with a tie belt. May be selected in a green, red or blue design. Sizes, 13, 15 and 17, $5.75.

42M61 Fine knife plaiting forms an integral part of this crepe de Chine frock especially designed for a junior miss. A band of plain material intersects the plaiting of the skirt just below the waistline and is finished with a buckled bow to match the one on the belt. The colours offered are athenia rose, Queen blue, gooseberry green or white. Sizes, 13, 15 and 17, $16.50.

38M75 This close-fitting peanut straw hat rolls off the face and is banded with grosgrain. The simulated tucking in front strikes a new note. Black, navy or green, $6.00.

42M62 Details that are particularly suited to a junior miss are evidenced in the turn-over collar, soft tie and unusual belt on this frock of radium silk printed in a pleasing all-over design. Plaits which start at the shoulders and stitched at the waistline give the skirt fulness. Green, navy, French blue or red with white trimming. Sizes, 13, 15 and 17, $16.50.

42M63 For the active junior miss there is a practical silk broadcloth frock of a sports character. The tailored V-neck and the sleeves introduce contrasting band trimming which is very effective. The belt is of self-material and the skirt shows three inverted plaits in front. Frock may be chosen in peach, blue, green or gold. Sizes, 13, 15 and 17, $12.75.

34M103 A becoming poke shape of fancy straw features the ripple brim and two-tone colour scheme. The brim is faced with silk. Sand, all-white or French blue, $3.75.

Scale of sizes of Junior Misses' Dresses

Sizes:	13	15	17
Bust:	32	33½	35½
Lengths:	39	40	41

| 71M75
$9.75 | 71M76
$9.85 | 71M77
$10.50 | 71M78
$12.00 | 34M102
$9.00(Hat) |

Fashion Experts Turn Their Talents to Cotton Creations

71M75 The practicability of this frock is evident since it is made of white dimity, a fabric that retains its freshness and always appears cool in the warm weather. The dotted trimming bands introduce a note of colour. Plaits appear at the front of the skirt. Pearl buttons suffice as trimming. The bands may have blue, black or red dots on white ground. Sizes, 16 to 20, also 36 to 42, $9.75.

71M76 A more delightful frock for the summer wardrobe could not be imagined than this one of embroidered cotton voile. It is distinctly of the youthful type, made in one piece, with plaits, adding fulness to the front of skirt. Tiny Val. lace ruffles adorn the collar and pockets which are further augmented by ribbon bows. The daintiest of colours are offered—rose background embroidered in blue and white, French blue with rose and white or white with French blue and rose embroidery. Sizes, 14 to 20, $9.85.

71M77 A decidedly wearable dress of cotton voile is developed in plain grey with French blue, navy with bisque or bisque with light leather colour. The skirt is plaited across the front and the back is plain. Tucks border the bosom front which is outlined with a double row of hemstitching. Tucks also trim the cuffs. Sizes, 36 to 46, $10.50.

71M78 Printed cotton crepe with a black tracery pattern against a white ground and trimming details of plain white make a very effective combination for this type of summer frock. Or if you prefer you may have it in Copen with a tan pattern, in which case the trimming details will be tan. The collar is convertible and thus can be worn high or low. Tunic at front of skirt. Sizes, 36 to 46, $12.00.

34M102 To successfully complete the summer costume this large black transparent hair hat will be needed. A band of grosgrain and satin encircles the crown, $9.00.

Scale of sizes of Women's and Misses' Cotton Dresses

Sizes:	14	16	18	20	
Lengths:	41	42	43	44	inches
Sizes:	36	38-40	42-44	46	
Lengths:	44	45	46	47	

Meet the Breakers in Smart Attire

78M50 Two-piece swimming suit with navy blue flannel trunks and an all-white wool jersey shirt. Sizes, 34 to 40, $5.75.
78M50A May also be had with jersey shirt striped in white-and-green, white-and-Copen, or white-and-red, $5.75.
78M51 Diving cap of heavy rubber in white, black or grey, 50c.
78M52 Novelty cretonne bathing bag in bright colourings, $1.85.
78M53 Wool jersey rib-knit swimming suit in black, Copen, Kelly green or navy. Sizes, 34 to 44, $3.95.
78M54 Novelty rubber cap in assorted colours, 45c.

78M51
50¢(Cap)

78M50
$5.75

78M54
45¢(Cap)

78M55
$2.90(Shoes)

78M53
$3.95

78M58
$2.50(Cap)

78M61
$1.25(Cap)

78M52
$1.85

78M56
$15.75

78M57
$14.75(Cape)

78M59
$6.75

78M60
$2.95(Coat,

78M56

78M55 Effective to wear on the beach are these black satin bathing slippers with satin ribbon lacings and rubber soles. Sizes, 3, 4, 5, 6 and 7, $2.90.

78M56 At Deauville and other smart watering-places Patou's new bathing suit featuring the U-shaped decollete at the back was enthusiastically received. Here we have copied it in French jersey and present it in these colours: pink, orchid, yellow, hydrangea blue or black. Separate trunks to match are included. Sizes, 16 and 18; also 36 to 40, $15.75.

78M57 To cover the above suit with chic there is this cape of French jersey to match. Pink, orchid, yellow, hydrangea blue or black, $14.75.

78M58 Rubberized moire bathing hat in purple, rose, yellow, blue or black, $2.50.

78M59 A simply fashioned bathing suit of black jacquard poplin. Sizes, 34 to 44, $6.75. **78M59A** Same model made of gayly printed silk in various designs, $7 50. (*Combination to be worn with this suit is described in No. 78M78 on opposite page.*)

78M60 A popular type of beach coat is made of cretonne showing a colourful flower pattern. Sizes, small, medium or large, $2.95.

78M61 Hand-painted rubber triangle bandanna in Copen blue, red, green or black, $1 25.

Bask in Beach Sunshine
Correctly Outfitted

78M65 This misses' one-piece wool jersey swimming suit looks as though it were two-piece because of the plain colour trunks and striped top. Comes in green, red or Copen blue. Sizes, 8, 10, 12, 14, $3.75.

78M66 A cunning novelty bathing bag with slide fastening, $4 10.

78M67 Most attractive is this black bathing suit, which may be taffeta or satin, as you prefer, piped with Copen, red or black. Sizes, 34 to 44, $5.90. (*Combination to be worn with this suit is described in No. 78M78*)

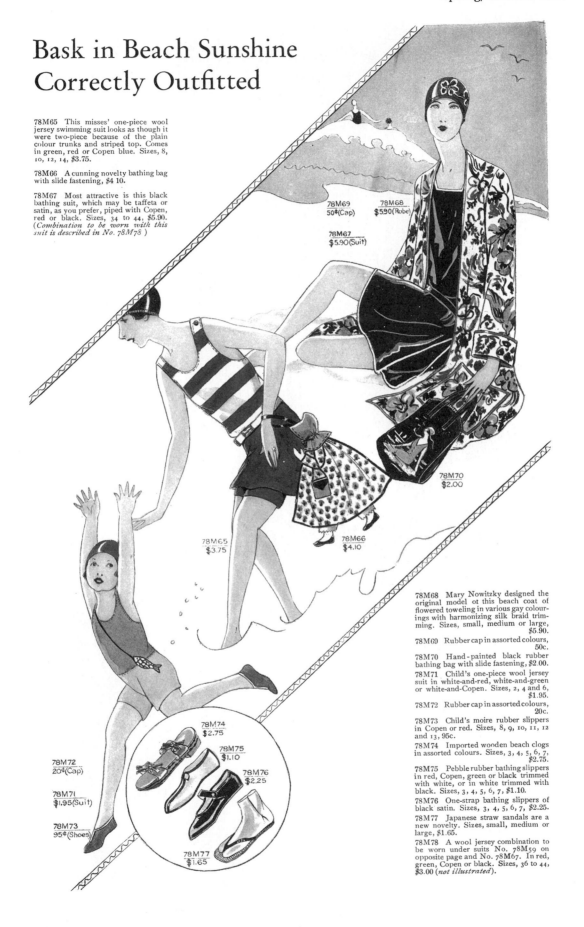

78M69
50¢(Cap)

78M68
$5.90(Robe)

78M67
$5.90(Suit)

78M70
$2.00

78M65
$3.75

78M66
$4.10

78M72
20¢(Cap)

78M71
$1.95(Suit)

78M73
95¢(Shoes)

78M74
$2.75

78M75
$1.10

78M76
$2.25

78M77
$1.65

78M68 Mary Nowitzky designed the original model ot this beach coat of flowered toweling in various gay colourings with harmonizing silk braid trimming. Sizes, small, medium or large, $5.90.

78M69 Rubber cap in assorted colours, 50c.

78M70 Hand - painted black rubber bathing bag with slide fastening, $2.00.

78M71 Child's one-piece wool jersey suit in white-and-red, white-and-green or white-and-Copen. Sizes, 2, 4 and 6, $1.95.

78M72 Rubber cap in assorted colours, 20c.

78M73 Child's moire rubber slippers in Copen or red. Sizes, 8, 9, 10, 11, 12 and 13, 95c.

78M74 Imported wooden beach clogs in assorted colours. Sizes, 3, 4, 5, 6, 7, $2.75.

78M75 Pebble rubber bathing slippers in red, Copen, green or black trimmed with white, or in white trimmed with black. Sizes, 3, 4, 5, 6, 7, $1.10.

78M76 One-strap bathing slippers of black satin. Sizes, 3, 4, 5, 6, 7, $2.25.

78M77 Japanese straw sandals are a new novelty. Sizes, small, medium or large, $1.65.

78M78 A wool jersey combination to be worn under suits No. 78M59 on opposite page and No. 78M67. In red, green, Copen or black. Sizes, 36 to 44, $3.00 (*not illustrated*).

59S35 One-piece chiffon dinner dress shades in ombre effect from a light tone in the cape blouse through intermediate shades to dark at the bottom of the tiered skirt, which boasts the smart longer-in-back hemline. Large chiffon bow at the side. Light to deep fuchsia; light to Prado (powder) blue; maize to sunflower; also in all-white. Silk crepe slip. Sizes, 14 to 20, $39.75

59S36 The taffeta bouffant frock for evening is of utmost style importance. This charming model has a large bow at the hipline in the Louiseboulanger manner, fastened with organdie flowers and lined with contrasting colour, which also faces the wide-scalloped, dipping hem. In black faced with jade; coral with Prado blue; honeydew with Romance (peach shades). Sizes, 14 to 20, $39.75

18S48
$4.90

18S48 Tiny silver and gold coloured metal beads are combined in various attractive designs in small evening bags. 4 x 5¼ in., $4.90

59S35
$39.75

59S36
$39.75°

Expressing the Youthful Spirit

59S37 Printed chiffon in a maze of colour on a beige or navy ground makes a fascinating frock for summer gayeties. The very full circular skirt is picoted around the bottom and joined to the blouse with stitched bands of material. The adjustable sash may be tied in front or on the side. Complete with matching handkerchief scarf and nude crepe de Chine slip. Sizes, 14 to 20, $35.00

59S38 This chiffon frock has a decided bias for chic, following the diagonal line of fashion in the cut of its neckline, in the oblique tucking of the blouse and in the spiral drape of its girdle. The skirt has sunburst plaiting all around and the waist, attached at the beltline to a matching silk crepe slip, blouses softly over the girdle. Cornflower blue, jade green or black. Sizes, 14 to 20, $35.00

59S39 Chiffon and silk lace join forces to make this individual afternoon frock which bases its claim of importance on its chiffon-edged circular tiers, its side flare, falling below the hemline, and the soft bias fold which frames the bateau neck and ties in a bow on the shoulder. Matching silk foundation. Black or beige. Sizes, 14 to 20, $45

59S37
$35.00

59S38
$35.00

59S39
$45.00

Prints and Solid Colours Find Equal Favour

59S44   Two diagonal lines of hand fagoting trim the blouse of this misses' two-piece crepe satin frock, which has a shirred tab at the hip-line fastened with a stone-set pin. The straight-line skirt, with a restrained front drape, shirred at the top, is attached to a bodice of self-material. Comes in black or Mother-Goose (tan). Sizes, 14 to 20, $29.75

59S45   A plaited frill with a double edging of light and dark contrasting colour, matched by the edging on the bottom of the skirt, is the style point of this two-piece frock of printed silk crepe. Dark suede belt. Cluster side-plaited skirt on bodice top. Red, navy or Flemish (medium) blue grounds. Prints may vary. Sizes, 14, 16, 18, 20, $29.75

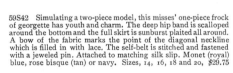

34S77
$5.75 Hat.

59S44
$29.75 Dress

34S84
$9.75 Hat.

59S45
$29.75 Dress

59S42
$29.75 Dress.

59S42   Simulating a two-piece model, this misses' one-piece frock of georgette has youth and charm. The deep hip band is scalloped around the bottom and the full skirt is sunburst plaited all around. A bow of the fabric marks the point of the diagonal neckline which is filled in with lace. The self-belt is stitched and fastened with a jeweled pin. Attached to matching silk slip. Monet (royal) blue, rose bisque (tan) or navy. Sizes, 14, 16, 18 and 20, $29.75

59S43   An all-over geometric print shading from colour to colour in ombre effect is used for this distinctive two-piece crepe de Chine frock. The loose scarf collar, tying in the back, the cuffs and bottom of the blouse are edged with black. The plaited skirt on a bodice top has a pointed hemline. Prints shade through orchid, blue, gold and rose. Or through orchid, apricot, blue, grey and green. Prints may vary. Sizes, 14, 16, 18 and 20, $29.75

34S77   Crochet straw hat shown on page 47

34S84   Crochet straw hat shown on page 47

34S86   Large black milan straw with grosgrain ribbon band, $11.50

Scale of sizes for Misses' Dresses:

Sizes	14	16	18	20	years
Bust measurements	32	34	36	38	inches
Length of dress from center back of neckline to hem of skirt	40	41	42	43	inches

In ordering Misses' garments, please specify size usually selected, 14, 16, 18 or 20 years, in addition to bust and length measurements

34S86
$11.50 Hat.

59S43
$29.75 Dress.

For Miss Junior

42J62
$5.75

42J63
$16.75

42J64
$9.75

42J62 Miss Junior never knows an awkward age, for she dresses smartly in such well-designed frocks as this dotted Normandy voile made in a one-piece belted style with surplice collar of imported white organdie edged with fagoting and contrasting binding. White with red or green dots; or navy blue with white dots. Sizes, 13, 15 and 17. Special, $5.75

42J63 A very charming one-piece frock for Miss Junior is made of georgette with detachable collar and cuffs of fine plaiting. The skirt is double box-plaited all around. In navy with white collar edged with red and navy; or in tan with tan collar edged with flame. Complete with slip. Sizes, 13, 15 and 17, $16.75

42J64 The stripes of this washable silk broadcloth are interestingly manipulated to give distinction to a sleeveless frock for Miss Junior. Complete with contrasting silk tie and suede belt. Rose, copen or green predominating. Sizes, 13, 15 and 17, $9.75

WOMEN'S SILK FROCKS

55J116 The growing popularity of sun-tanned arms makes this sleeveless frock of washable Honan silk a desirable model for spectator wear as well as for sports. A diagonal neckline with button trimming, sunray tucking on the blouse and plaiting in the front of the skirt add appreciably to the frock's attractiveness. Rose, green or white. Sizes, 16 and 18; 38 to 40, $7.85
55J117 This attractive, semi-tailored frock is made of an unweighted, sheer silk crepe that is very cool and comfortable for warm summer weather, and the polka dot print is exceedingly smart. The collar and ends of the soft bow tie are made of white silk and the skirt front is plaited to a V-shaped yoke. Navy ground with white or tan dots. Sizes, 16 and 18; 36 to 44, $7.85
34J137 Agnes slashes the brim of the felt hat from which this model is copied, and crosses the points against the crown. Black or white, $7.50

34J137
$7.50 Hat

55J117
$7.85 Dress

55J116
$7.85

Scale of sizes of Junior Misses' Dresses			
Sizes :	13	15	17
Bust:	32	33½	35½
Lengths:	39	40	41

Coat Fashions for Women and Misses

34J134
$6.50 Hat

34J131
$4.50 Hat

34J137
$7.50 Hat

63J75
$55.00 Coat

63J76
$15.00 Coat

67J77
$25.00 Coat

34J138
$10.00

34J132
$10.00

34J131 Felt hat described on page 9
34J134 Felt hat described on page 14
34J137 Felt hat described on page 7

	Lengths of Women's Coats			
Sizes:	36	38-40	42-44	46
Lengths:	43	44	45	46
	Scale of sizes of Misses Coats			
Sizes:	14	16	18	20	years
Lengths:	40	41	42	43	inches

63J75 A travel coat of great becomingness and unusual distinction is fashioned of a very soft camel's hair and wool material in an indistinct pin-check weave and finished with a generous collar of deep, rich brown beaver. The diagonal weave of the selvedge is used in the French manner to trim the fronts and the smart shaped cuffs. This is an outstanding value that should not be overlooked. Tan only. Silk lined throughout. Misses' sizes, 14, 16, 18 and 20, $55.00. 67J75 Same coat in women's sizes, 36 to 46, $55.00

63J76 This unlined summer sports coat of flannel is an exceedingly smart and well-tailored garment despite its modest price. Made on slim, youthful lines and simply trimmed with narrow tucks, which also appear in the center back, it can be worn on many occasions. Note the interesting detail on the pockets and the nonchalant air given by the narrow belt which may be omitted if desired. White only. Misses' sizes, 14, 16, 18 and 20, $15.00. 67J76 In women's sizes, 36 to 46, $15.00

67J77 A delightful coat for town or travel is made of a supple tweed, the stitched roll collar permitting the use of a fur scarf when desired. In tan or grey lined throughout with matching silk crepe. Women's sizes, 36 to 46, $25.00. 63J77 Misses' sizes, 14, 16, 18 and 20, in tan or specially ordered in grey, $25.00. 67J77A Same coat in brameena (a dressier kashmir fabric) in middy blue (light navy) or black. Women's sizes, 36 to 46, $25.00. 63J77A Same coat in brameena, misses' sizes, 14, 16, 18 and 20, $25.00

34J132 This large Paillasson straw hat in natural colour with binding and band of black or navy blue grosgrain ribbon is adapted from an Agnes model. This type of hat will be worn all summer, $10.00

34J138 Stitched taffeta silk, the newest of smart hat materials, makes this clever little cloche which has its brim uniquely folded in the back and trimmed with a gilt metal figurine and two dogs. Navy or sand, $10.00

73S50
$45.00 Fur.

69S35
$39.00 Suit.

34S90
$6.75 Hat.

69S36
$59.00
Ensemble

73S51
$38.00 Fur.

69S37
$25.00 Suit.

34S91
$11.50 Hat.

69S38
$59.00
Ensemble

Suits and Ensembles Increase in Favour

69S36

69S35 This woman's suit of twill, smartly tailored and bound with silk braid, is made with the straight wrap-around skirt and single-breasted jacket that will be so popular this spring. In navy blue or oxford. Sizes, 36 to 44. Can be specially ordered in black, $39.00

69S36 The ensemble, more important this season than ever, is here developed in a misses' model of navy twill with seven-eighths coat and box-plaited skirt on bodice top. Surplice style blouse of beige silk crepe; also boy blue blouse. Sizes, 14 to 20, $59.00

69S37 An attractive misses' suit of youthful lines has a single-breasted box coat with silk bound pocket flaps and silk banding and button trim at the sides. Wrap-around skirt. Comes in tan tweed, oxford twill, navy twill; 14, 16, 18, 20. Specially priced, $25.00

69S38

69S38 Detail and careful workmanship characterize this becoming ensemble which includes a seven-eighths coat and front-plaited skirt of kashmir and a silk crepe blouse made with the becoming V-neck. Skirt has bodice top. Navy with beige blouse or all-tan. May be specially ordered in black with beige blouse; 36 to 42, $59.00

73S50 This brown fox scarf adds chic to the spring suit or ensemble, $45.00. Also fox scarfs in white and delicate shades of beige, grey, sand or cocoa at $75.00; $85.00; $110.00 and up

73S51 A pointed fox scarf is exceedingly smart for spring, $38.00 An extensive collection of scarfs, including pointed, black, brown or natural red fox at $38.00; $45.00; $55.00; $65.00; $75.00 and up

67S40
$45.00

67S41
$68.00

67S42
$58.00

34S78
$9.50 Hat.

67S43
$55.00 Coat.

Women's Coats Inspired by Paris

67S40   A smart standing collar of dyed squirrel fitting close to the back of the neck increases the becomingness of this straight-line kashmir coat which is distinguished by unique seaming both front and back. Silk lined. Black, tan or navy blue. May be specially ordered in grey with grey squirrel. Sizes, 36 to 46, $45.00

67S41   A sophisticated coat for formal wear is fashioned of brameena (a soft kashmir fabric) with slot seaming in front and back and on the sleeves. Silk lined. In black with white ermine collar; tan with beige ermine; or black with beige ermine. 36 to 46, $68.00

67S42   A becoming kit fox collar gives richness to this ultra-smart coat of imported tweed combining diagonal with horizontal lines in a very distinguished effect. Lined with silk crepe. Comes in tan-and-brown mixture or in grey mixture. Sizes, 36 to 46, $58.00

67S43   Adapted from a Vionnet model, this coat of kashmir possesses unusual style distinction, for the graceful scarf and intricate seaming are of satin, the collar is of dyed squirrel, and the boutonniere of French glass flowers. Silk lined. Black or tan. May be specially ordered in grey with grey squirrel. 36 to 46, $55.00

Lengths of Women's Coats

Sizes:	36-38	40-42	44-46
Lengths:	43	44	45

Coats and Ensembles for the Junior Miss

42S40 A suit for Miss Junior, as smart as it is practical, is fashioned of tan and brown tweed mixture or of navy cheviot. Wrap-around skirt; notch-collared jacket, double-breasted. Sizes, 13, 15, 17, $19.75. **42S40A** Tailored full-length coat to match, lined throughout with soft silk, which may be worn separately, $19.75. **42S40B** Three-piece ensemble, $39.50

38S50 Curved tucks relieve the severity of this brimmed hat of fine quality navy blue or almond green felt. The simple band is of belting ribbon, $4.50

42S41 A smartly tailored double-breasted coat for the Miss Junior is fashioned of soft-finished tan and brown tweed. Tailored cuffs, set-in sleeves and narrow belt with bone buckle. Lined with silk throughout. Sizes, 13, 15, 17, $17.50

38S51 This youthful cloche of felt has a crown encircled by tucks. French blue with matching ribbon or beige with brown trimming. A smart model, $4.50

42S42 Splendid quality navy blue cheviot with a slightly wider wale is used for a smart coat for the junior miss. The scarf collar is of tan silk crepe to match the lining. Sizes, 13, 15, 17, $25.00

42S43 Miss Junior will be very smart indeed in this ensemble of pin-checked tweed. The one-piece frock has cord tucking and buttoned tabs in front and back and a plaited skirt section. Full-length coat lined with matching silk may be worn separately. Tan, green or grey. Sizes, 13, 15 and 17, $29.50

42S44 Miss Junior will step gayly forth in this dressy coat of kashmir which boasts the smart scarf collar. The embroidery on collar, cuffs and scarf ends done in contrasting shades gives the desired touch of colour; natural (tan) or almond green. Sizes, 13, 15, 17, $25.00

38S50 $4.50

38S51 $4.50

38S50 $4.50

38S51 $4.50

42S40 $19.75 Suit.

42S40A $19.75 Separate Coat.

42S40B $39.50 Ensemble

42S41 $17.50

42S42 $25.00

42S43 $29.50

42S44 $25.00

Smart Frocks for the Junior Miss

42S47 Combining youthful becomingness with the sophistication demanded by Miss Junior, this two-piece frock of flat crepe is an unusual value. The hand-hemstitched trim on the blouse is outlined by a cord tuck and the bodice-topped skirt is box-plaited in front. Tan, Lucerne blue or almond green. Sizes, 13, 15 and 17, $10.75

42S48 The nonchalant handkerchief scarf of the printed silk crepe that makes the skirt is the style feature of this two-piece frock for Miss Junior. The flat crepe blouse is navy, with a skirt having a tan ground in the print, or copen with copen print, or tan with tan print. Sizes, 13, 15 and 17, $16.75

42S49 Soft-textured, pin-checked worsted is used for a two-piece frock for Miss Junior. The blouse has chevron tucking both back and front, a novelty belt and printed silk kerchief in the pocket. The skirt is group-plaited across the front on bodice top. Tan, blue or green. Sizes, 13, 15 and 17, $16.75

42S47
$10.75

42S48
$16.75

42S49
$16.75

42S50 A smart confetti-printed crepe de Chine fashions an attractive frock for Miss Junior. Silk fagoting and a narrow two-tone border of silk crepe trim the bottom and the cuffs. Flounce is finely plaited across the front. Navy or tan ground printed in a varicoloured design. Sizes, 13, 15 and 17, $16.75

42S51 The blouse of a heavy flat crepe frock for Miss Junior has overlapping tucks around the hips, and a self-coloured suede belt. Skirt, on bodice top, is plaited across the front. Rose beige with nude trimming, Lucerne blue with shrimp or navy with shrimp. Sizes, 13, 15 and 17, $16.75

Scale of sizes of Junior Misses' Dresses

Sizes:	13	15	17
Bust:	32	33½	35½
Lengths:	39	40	41

To FACILITATE *the prompt and correct filling of orders, it is suggested that the order blank be used in every instance possible. Additional order blanks will be sent upon request*

42S50
$16.75

42S51
$16.75

Fashionable Shoes for Smart Young Feet

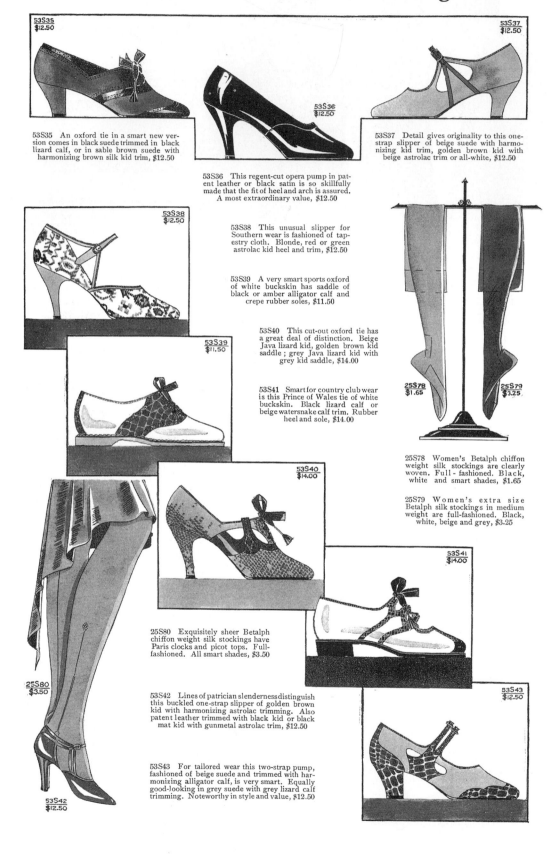

53S35 An oxford tie in a smart new version comes in black suede trimmed in black lizard calf, or in sable brown suede with harmonizing brown silk kid trim, $12.50

53S36 This regent-cut opera pump in patent leather or black satin is so skillfully made that the fit of heel and arch is assured. A most extraordinary value, $12.50

53S37 Detail gives originality to this one-strap slipper of beige suede with harmonizing kid trim, golden brown kid with beige astrolac trim or all-white, $12.50

53S38 This unusual slipper for Southern wear is fashioned of tapestry cloth. Blonde, red or green astrolac kid heel and trim, $12.50

53S39 A very smart sports oxford of white buckskin has saddle of black or amber alligator calf and crepe rubber soles, $11.50

53S40 This cut-out oxford tie has a great deal of distinction. Beige Java lizard kid, golden brown kid saddle; grey Java lizard kid with grey kid saddle, $14.00

53S41 Smart for country club wear is this Prince of Wales tie of white buckskin. Black lizard calf or beige watersnake calf trim. Rubber heel and sole, $14.00

25S78 Women's Betalph chiffon weight silk stockings are clearly woven. Full-fashioned. Black, white and smart shades, $1.65

25S79 Women's extra size Betalph silk stockings in medium weight are full-fashioned. Black, white, beige and grey, $3.25

25S80 Exquisitely sheer Betalph chiffon weight silk stockings have Paris clocks and picot tops. Full-fashioned. All smart shades, $3.50

53S42 Lines of patrician slenderness distinguish this buckled one-strap slipper of golden brown kid with harmonizing astrolac trimming. Also patent leather trimmed with black kid or black mat kid with gunmetal astrolac trim, $12.50

53S43 For tailored wear this two-strap pump, fashioned of beige suede and trimmed with harmonizing alligator calf, is very smart. Equally good-looking in grey suede with grey lizard calf trimming. Noteworthy in style and value, $12.50

Footwear That Leads the Fashion Parade

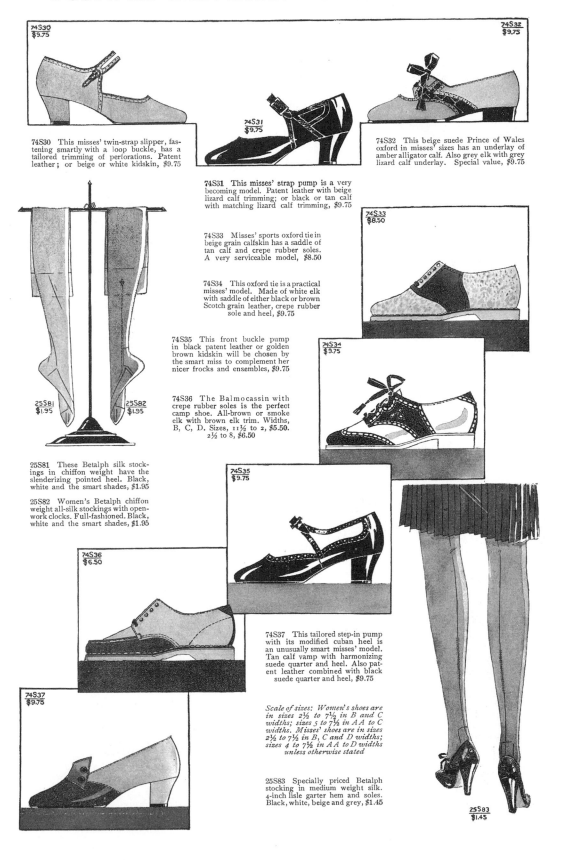

74S30 $9.75

74S31 $9.75

74S32 $9.75

74S33 $8.50

74S34 $9.75

74S35 $9.75

74S36 $6.50

74S37 $9.75

25S81 $1.95

25S82 $1.95

25S83 $1.45

74S30 This misses' twin-strap slipper, fastening smartly with a loop buckle, has a tailored trimming of perforations. Patent leather; or beige or white kidskin, $9.75

74S31 This misses' strap pump is a very becoming model. Patent leather with beige lizard calf trimming; or black or tan calf with matching lizard calf trimming, $9.75

74S32 This beige suede Prince of Wales oxford in misses' sizes has an underlay of amber alligator calf. Also grey elk with grey lizard calf underlay. Special value, $9.75

74S33 Misses' sports oxford tie in beige grain calfskin has a saddle of tan calf and crepe rubber soles. A very serviceable model, $8.50

74S34 This oxford tie is a practical misses' model. Made of white elk with saddle of either black or brown Scotch grain leather, crepe rubber sole and heel, $9.75

74S35 This front buckle pump in black patent leather or golden brown kidskin will be chosen by the smart miss to complement her nicer frocks and ensembles, $9.75

74S36 The Balmocassin with crepe rubber soles is the perfect camp shoe. All-brown or smoke elk with brown elk trim. Widths, B, C, D. Sizes, 11½ to 2, $5.50. 2½ to 8, $6.50

25S81 These Betalph silk stockings in chiffon weight have the slenderizing pointed heel. Black, white and the smart shades, $1.95

25S82 Women's Betalph chiffon weight all-silk stockings with open-work clocks. Full-fashioned. Black, white and the smart shades, $1.95

74S37 This tailored step-in pump with its modified cuban heel is an unusually smart misses' model. Tan calf vamp with harmonizing suede quarter and heel. Also patent leather combined with black suede quarter and heel, $9.75

Scale of sizes: Women's shoes are in sizes 2½ to 7½ in B and C widths; sizes 5 to 7½ in A A to C widths. Misses' shoes are in sizes 2½ to 7½ in B, C and D widths; sizes 4 to 7½ in A A to D widths unless otherwise stated

25S83 Specially priced Betalph stocking in medium weight silk. 4-inch lisle garter hem and soles. Black, white, beige and grey, $1.45

The Chic Hat to Crown a Spring Ensemble

34S75 This clever felt cloche in the Descat manner is interestingly treated at the side and finished with a new double headed pin. The colours are black or beige, $9.75

18S30 Gold-plated necklace in new link effect with square imitation jade or lapis stone mounted in the center, $6.00

34S76 An inexpensive hat of bengaline silk has a semi-large brim which rolls up at the back. Grosgrain ribbon band and trimming. Colours are sand or navy blue, $5.50

18S31 For the smart costume, a 6o-inch rope of dull gold-coloured beads, knotted between each bead, is very effective, $2.90

34S77 Crochet straw develops this smart hat of becoming shape trimmed with grosgrain ribbon band and binding. In navy blue or almond green with jungle green, $5.75

14S25 Crepe de Chine square in maize, beige, copen or green, hand painted in contrasting colours. Also white with black, $2.95

34S80 Here is a small felt cloche that duplicates the chic of a Descat hat with tucking and grosgrain trimming. Grey or beige with brown, $4.95

34S81 Velvet geraniums in burnt orange or red with green leaves are smart, 65c.

34S82 Close-fitting hat of bengaline silk featuring a stitched brim, grosgrain ribbon trimming and buckle ornament. Colours, sand or navy blue, $3.75

34S83 To wear with afternoon costumes choose this natural colour orchid, 70c.

18S32 Brilliant rhinestone hat or shoulder pin of unusual originality, $3.00

34S78 The extreme cut of this felt hat is typical of the millinery mode and of Descat from whose model it is copied. Comes in sand or black, $9.50

34S79 A bunch of violets in natural or white will add interest to a tailleur. Special, 45c.

34S84 Reboux designed the original of this crochet straw hat having a brim that turns off the face with clever tucks held with a smart pin. White or black, $9.75

34S85 Two gardenias are allied to make this boutonniere. White, maize, sand, 45c.

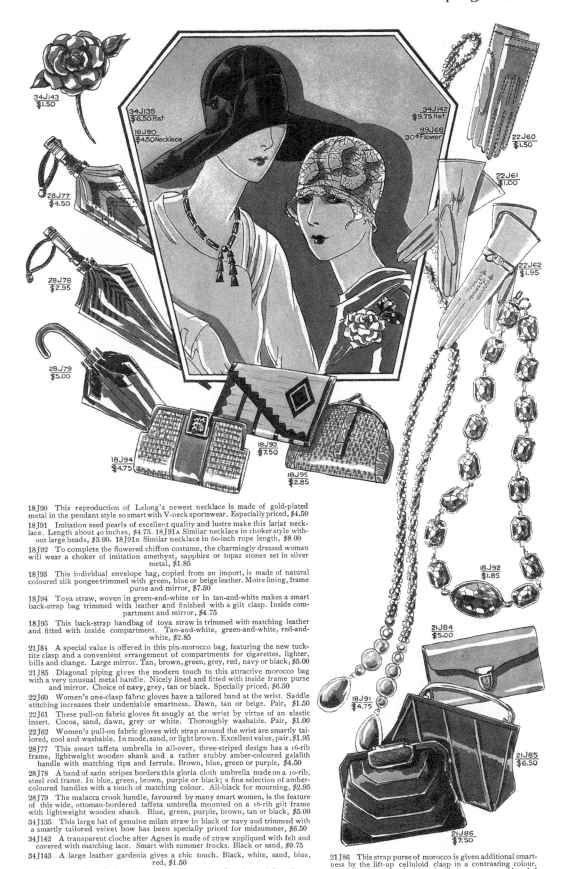

34J143
$1.50

34J135
$6.50 Hat

18J90
$4.50 Necklace

34J142
$9.75 Hat

89J68
30¢ Flower

22J60
$1.50

22J61
$1.00

28J77
$4.50

22J62
$1.95

28J78
$2.95

28J79
$5.00

18J93
$7.50

18J94
$4.75

18J95
$2.85

18J92
$1.85

21J84
$5.00

18J91
$4.75

21J85
$6.50

21J86
$7.50

18J90 This reproduction of Lelong's newest necklace is made of gold-plated metal in the pendant style so smart with V-neck sportswear. Especially priced, $4.50

18J91 Imitation seed pearls of excellent quality and lustre make this lariat necklace. Length about 40 inches, $4.75. 18J91A Similar necklace in choker style without large beads, $3.00. 18J91B Similar necklace in 60-inch rope length, $8.00

18J92 To complete the flowered chiffon costume, the charmingly dressed woman will wear a choker of imitation amethyst, sapphire or topaz stones set in silver metal, $1.85

18J93 This individual envelope bag, copied from an import, is made of natural coloured silk pongee trimmed with green, blue or beige leather. Moire lining, frame purse and mirror, $7.50

18J94 Toya straw, woven in green-and-white or in tan-and-white makes a smart back-strap bag trimmed with leather and finished with a gilt clasp. Inside compartment and mirror, $4.75

18J95 This back-strap handbag of toya straw is trimmed with matching leather and fitted with inside compartment. Tan-and-white, green-and-white, red-and-white, $2.85

21J84 A special value is offered in this pin-morocco bag, featuring the new tucktite clasp and a convenient arrangement of compartments for cigarettes, lighter, bills and change. Large mirror. Tan, brown, green, grey, red, navy or black, $5.00

21J85 Diagonal piping gives the modern touch to this attractive morocco bag with a very unusual metal handle. Nicely lined and fitted with inside frame purse and mirror. Choice of navy, grey, tan or black. Specially priced, $6.50

22J60 Women's one-clasp fabric gloves have a tailored band at the wrist. Saddle stitching increases their undeniable smartness. Dawn, tan or beige. Pair, $1.50

22J61 These pull-on fabric gloves fit snugly at the wrist by virtue of an elastic insert. Cocoa, sand, dawn, grey or white. Thoroughly washable. Pair, $1.00

22J62 Women's pull-on fabric gloves with strap around the wrist are smartly tailored, cool and washable. In mode, sand, or light brown. Excellent value, pair, $1.95

28J77 This smart taffeta umbrella in all-over, three-striped design has a 16-rib frame, lightweight wooden shank and a rather stubby amber-coloured galalith handle with matching tips and ferrule. Brown, blue, green or purple, $4.50

28J78 A band of satin stripes borders this gloria cloth umbrella made on a 10-rib, steel rod frame. In blue, green, brown, purple or black; a fine selection of amber-coloured handles with a touch of matching colour. All-black for mourning, $2.95

28J79 The malacca crook handle, favoured by many smart women, is the feature of this wide, ottoman-bordered taffeta umbrella mounted on a 16-rib gilt frame with lightweight wooden shank. Blue, green, purple, brown, tan or black, $5.00

34J135 This large hat of genuine milan straw in black or navy and trimmed with a smartly tailored velvet bow has been specially priced for midsummer, $6.50

34J142 A transparent cloche after Agnes is made of straw appliqued with felt and covered with matching lace. Smart with summer frocks. Black or sand, $9.75

34J143 A large leather gardenia gives a chic touch. Black, white, sand, blue, red, $1.50

89J68 Imported gardenia with bud comes in sand, red, apricot, pink, maize or white, 30c.

21J86 This strap purse of morocco is given additional smartness by the lift-up celluloid clasp in a contrasting colour. Nicely lined and fitted with an inside frame purse and beveled mirror. Comes in navy, grey, tan or black, $7.50

A Smart Alliance of Fabrics and Colours

34J132
$10.00 Hat

8J92
$25.00 Dress

34J139
$5.50 Hat

8J93
$19.75 Dress

34J134
$6.50 Hat

8J94
$25.00 Dress

8J92   Very smart indeed, and also very practical is this two-piece cardigan ensemble which includes a front-plaited jersey skirt attached to a dotted silk crepe blouse, and a matching jersey cardigan. In navy blue with blue blouse and white polka dots; or in fallow tan with tan blouse and brown polka dots. Equally suitable for summertime and early fall wear. Sizes, 14 to 18 and 38 to 40, $25.00

34J132 Straw hat, described on page 8

8J93   A two-piece silk crepe sports dress of unusual chic has a round neck with separate scarf throw and a front-plaited skirt. The blouse, which is gathered under the belt on each side to give a snug-fitting hipline, has a yoke back with an inverted plait on each side. Spark red bordered with black and white; orchid with purple and white; almond green bordered with black and white. Sizes, 14 to 20, $19.75

34J139 Felt hat, described on page 10

8J94   A most unusual costume that combines perfect taste with unique designing has a supple jersey blouse printed in softly blended colours in modernistic design and a canton crepe skirt plaited all around to a bodice top. The hipband is adjusted by a grosgrain ribbon lacing on the left side. The blouse is printed in tan, brown and blue tones and the skirt is a harmonizing tan shade. Sizes, 14 to 18; 38 and 40, $25.00

34J134 Felt hat, described on page 14

Scale of sizes of Women's and Misses' Sports Dresses

Sizes:	14	16	18	20	38	40	42	44
Lengths:	40	41	42	43	44	44	45	45

| 34J137 $7.50 Hat | 83J100 $8.75 Jacket | 83J101 $9.75 Skirt | 34J132 $10.00 Hat | 83J102 $22.75 Suit | 34J144 $5.00 Hat | 83J103 $5.75 Sweater | 83J104 $9.75 Skirt |

83J100 This wearable jacquette model sweater is knitted of zephyr yarn in a fancy all-over pattern, combining copen blue-and-white, tan-and-rust or white-and-black, and finished with a becoming roll collar, cuffs and pocket facings of solid colour to match. Can be worn as an extra wrap or with a separate skirt to make a smart sports ensemble. Sizes, 36 to 46, $8.75

83J101 This smart flannel skirt, attached to a band and made with a yoke top for greater flatness, has a kick-plait on each side and a plain back. Attractive with jacquette No. 83J100. White or tan. Sizes, 26 to 36, $9.75

83J102 The fashion importance of knitted sportswear makes this three-piece cardigan ensemble an excellent selection for the vacation wardrobe. The cardigan and skirt are of knitted tweed pattern and the long-sleeved jumper is a rayon and zephyr mixture in harmonizing colour. In marine blue-and-white tweed mixture; spruce green-and-white or white-and-black. Sizes, 14 to 18; 38 to 42, $22.75

34J132 Paillasson straw hat described on page 8

34J137 Felt hat described on page 7

34J144 Felt hat described on page 12

83J103 There will be many times during the summer when the smartest possible costume will be a knitted sweater and plaited silk skirt ensemble. This jumper of zephyr is finished at neck, sleeves and bottom with contrasting stripes. In white with grey-and-black stripes; tan with brown-and-white; or almond with darker green-and-white. Sizes, 34 to 42, $5.75

83J104 This washable silk crepe skirt, making a costume with jumper No. 83J103, is box-plaited across the front to a bodice top and the edge of each plait is held by tailored stitching. In white or tan. Sizes, 14 to 18; 38 to 42, $9.75

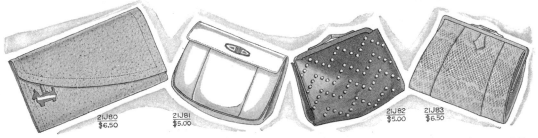

| 21J80 $6.50 | 21J81 $5.00 | 21J82 $5.00 | 21J83 $6.50 |

21J80 A smart diagonal flap, ornamented with a metal dog, is the modern note in this envelope of pig grain calf. Fitted with silk purse and mirror. Red, navy, tan, green or black; also in white kid, $6.50

21J81 The new frameless pouch bag sponsored by Paris is here developed in pin morocco and fastened with a fancy enameled clasp. Fitted with back strap, purse and mirror, and nicely lined. Tan, brown, grey, green, red, navy or black; also in white kid, $5.00

21J82 Metal nailheads, which distinguish the newest imports, stud this strap purse of smooth calfskin, fastened with metal clasp and fitted with frame purse and mirror. Navy, tan, beige, grey, red, green, black, $5.00

21J83 This smart strap purse in the new size is made of grey or tan pin morocco with front of genuine watersnake. Inside frame purse and mirror. Very specially priced, $6.50

34S75

83S76
$5.75

83S77
$19.75

83S78
$ 9.75

83S79
$ 9.75

Separate
Cardigans and
Sweater
Ensembles

83S80 B
$ 7.75
Cardigan

83S80A
$17.25
2 piece jumper & skirt

83S80
$25.00
3 piece ensemble

83S81
$16.75

83S76 This good-looking cardigan sweater of mohair yarn has
border and the tops of its pockets of striped mohair and rayon. Very
smart for sports. Lucerne blue, cocoa or black-and-white. 34 to 46, $5.75

83S77 This belted suede jacket with notched collar and slit pockets
is copied from an imported model giving you all the chic of the original at a much lower price. Green, grey or reindeer tan. 34 to 46, $19.75

83S78 This pull-over sweater of zephyr yarn makes a most attractive
sports costume when worn with a plaited silk skirt. Red or copen with
stripings of white; or peach beige with orange. Sizes, 14 to 18; 38, $9.75

83S79 This flat crepe skirt with narrow front and side plaitings is
made with bodice top. White, peach beige or black. Sizes, 14 to 18;
38 to 42, $9.75

83S80 This three-piece knitted sports suit includes a cardigan and
skirt of zephyr and a jumper of striped zephyr and rayon. The skirt
on an elastic band has two inverted plaits. Lucerne blue, French beige
or rose. Sizes, 34 to 42, $25.00. 83S80A May be specially ordered
as a two-piece suit of skirt and jumper, $17.25. 83S80B Separate
cardigan, $7.75

83S81 A two-piece knitted sports suit of mottled zephyr yarn has
darker bands applied in a very distinctive design. Skirt on bodice top.
French beige, Lucerne blue or Neptune green. Sizes, 34 to 42, $16.75

ARE you looking for a wedding present, a graduation gift or a birthday remembrance? Then ask our Gift Secretary to assist you. She will make selections for you and will see that each gift is attractively wrapped and stamped with the smart gold and black Altman Gift Seal

Knitted Sportswear Has Style Importance

83S70 Smart for golfing is this two-piece knitted frock of zephyr and rayon mixture. The pull-over sweater in shaded effect has the newest neck. Skirt on band. Lucerne blue, rose or Lanvin green. Sizes, 14 to 18; 38 to 40, $12.75

83S71 The all-over design which distinguishes this knitted cardigan is made by combining zephyr and rayon with very effective results. In Lucerne blue; Mother-Goose tan or Lanvin green. 34 to 46, $10.75

83S72 This unusual pull-over sweater of zephyr and rayon has the smart crew neck and novelty striping in modernistic effect across the front. Flame, almond green or Lucerne blue. Sizes, 34 to 40, $5.75

83S73 Very smart indeed is a knitted coat frock of silver-tone yarn in hairline stripe effect. Attractive pique collar and cuffs. In navy-and-silver, green-and-beige or brown-and-tan. Sizes, 36 to 46, $16.75

83S74 Again zephyr and rayon are combined for greater smartness in a pull-over sweater woven in an all-over diamond design and made with the interesting new neckline. Green-and-white, tan-and-white or white-and-black in grey effect. Sizes, 34 to 40, $8.75

83S75 This kashaline cloth skirt, box-plaited across the front to a bodice top, comes in green, grey or tan to harmonize with the colours of sweater No.83S74. Also smart with silk blouse; 34 to 40, $9.75

72 S 62
$6.95

72 S 63
$11.95

72 S 64
$4.95

72 S 66
$12.95

72 S 65
$5.95

72 S 67
$8.95

Robes Cleverly Designed

72S62 For lightness combined with warmth this lounging robe of wool albatross is ideal. Made with the popular side-tie closing and trimmed with bindings of matching satin. French blue, rose, pink or orchid. Sizes, 14 and 16; 36 to 44, $6.95

72S63 This mannish robe is made of flannel in a variety of stripings which feature rose or blue in assorted colour combinations. This is the type of robe that is especially favoured by girls at school. Sizes, 14, 16 and 18; 36 to 44, $11.95

72S64 This very smart but inexpensive negligee is made of boxloom (cotton) crepe in the convenient side-tie model. The deep collar, cuffs and pocket are elaborately embroidered. Rose, copen or orchid. Sizes, 14 and 16; 36 to 44, $4.95

72S65 This good quality terry cloth bathrobe in blazer stripings of gold-and-white, blue-and-white or red-and-white has a cord girdle and cord-finished pocket, cuffs, collar and front edges. Very practical. 14 and 16; 36 to 44, $5.95

72S66 This black satin lounging robe of a distinctive and bizarre attractiveness is bound and faced with gold cloth and the pockets are elaborately embroidered in a Chinese pattern with gold thread. Sizes, 14 and 16; 36 to 44, $12.95

72S67 An exceedingly dainty negligee that is quite suitable for a trousseau is made of good quality crepe de Chine with lace-trimmed pockets and triple rows of lace frills. Nile, coral or turquoise. Sizes, 14, 16 and 18; 36 to 40, $8.95

72S55

72S55
$10.95

72S56
$19.95

72S57
$11.95

14S40
$1.45

14S41
$1.00

72S58
$17.95

72S59
$22.50

Negligees of Feminine Loveliness

72S55 The pleasure of leisure hours is greatly augmented by such a lovely negligee as this one of fringed crepe de Chine made in a sleeveless, cape-back model. French blue, coral, nile or turquoise. Sizes, 14 and 16; 36 to 40, $10.95

72S56 A very distinguished negligee is this, made of lustrous black or French blue Chin-chin crepe, banded in three graded shades of harmonizing colour. Lined throughout with harmonizing Chin-chin crepe. Sizes, 14 and 16; 36 to 44, $19.95

72S57 Red, green or blue makes the facing and trimming on this arresting negligee of a crowded all-over printed design in bright colours on a black ground.   The material is a lustrous-finished satin. Sizes, 14 to 16; 36 to 44, $11.95

72S58 This fluffy feminine negligee designed for the petite type is made of printed georgette and lined throughout with crepe de Chine. Pink over pink, nile over pink, or white over pink with pastel flower sprays. Sizes 14, 16, 18, $17.95

72S59 An exquisite teagown copied from a model by Molyneux has wing draperies ot chiffon flowing over a crepe satin slip trimmed with cream thread lace.   Edges are finished with picoting. Light blue, nile or coral, 36 to 40, $22.50

14S40 Boudoir cap of satin trimmed with ribbon and net ruffles. In pink, blue, lavender, peach, rose or copen blue, $1.45

14S41 Satin boudoir cap trimmed with lace and ribbon. Pink, peach, lavender, blue, rose or copen, $1.00

Approved by the Fastidious

46S50 This Betalph milanese silk vest has pink and coral applique and binding. Comes in flesh only. Sizes, 34 to 42, $3.25

46S51 Betalph milanese silk bloomers have pink and coral appliques to match vest No. 46S50. Come in flesh only. Sizes, 5, 6, 7, $4.50

46S52 This Betalph glove silk gown in flesh, nile or peach, in the comfortable shoulder strap style, is lace trimmed. 15, 16 and 17, $5.90

48S130 A dance set of slim proportions is made of pink, nile or maize crepe de Chine. The bandeau and abbreviated panties, on a shaped front yoke, are trimmed with novel lace. Sizes, 32 to 36, 2-piece set, $3.25

48S131 An embroidered motif adds to the elaborateness of this lace-trimmed slip of good quality crepe de Chine. The plain hem is shadow-proof. Comes in pink or white. Sizes, 36 to 44, $5.75

48S132 An exquisite slip of high-grade radium silk owes its distinction to the motif of cut work embroidery which trims the front. Made with shadow-proof hem. Pink, white or beige. Sizes, 36 to 44, $7.95

48S133 Full-cut bloomers of crepe de Chine have petal ruffles faced with contrasting colour to match applique on side. Made with shaped front yoke. In flesh with coral or peach with orchid. Lengths, 23 and 25, $5.75. 48S133A Plain flesh crepe de Chine bloomers with elastic top and bottom. Lengths, 23, 25 and 27 inches, $2.95

48S134 This lovely crepe de Chine step-in chemise is effectively trimmed with deep-embroidered net lace and applique. A delightful gift for the girl graduate. White, peach or sweet pea. Sizes, 34 to 38, $7.95

48S135 This crepe de Chine slip for every-day wear has machine hemstitching in yoke effect and a shadow-proof hem. A highly practical model that comes in pink, white, beige or black. Sizes, 36 to 44, $3.95

48S136 This Paris-made crepe de Chine nightrobe is as lovely as only French lingerie decorated with hand embroidery, hemstitching and lace can be. Comes in pink, peach or nile. Sizes, 14, 15 and 16, $9.75

48S137 This pyjama ensemble has a coat and slip-over top of printed tub silk with red or blue background. The trousers and the trimming on the coat are made of black tub silk. Sizes, 36 to 40, $10.75

48S138 A deep yoke of net-lined Bretonne pattern lace is the feature of this crepe de Chine gown. The bottom is picoted in pointed scallops. Ribbon belt. In flesh or maize. Sizes, 14, 15, 16 and 17, $5.75

46S50 $3.25

48S130 $3.25 Set 2 pieces

46S51 $4.50

46S52 $5.90

48S133 $5.75

48S131 $5.75

48S132 $7.95

48S134 $7.95

48S135 $3.95

48S136 $9.75

48S138 $5.75

48S137 $10.75

17S73 Silk waist lining. Sizes, 34 to 44. Special value, $2.00

17S73 $2.00

New Models of Lovely Silk

48S140   This tailored gown of flesh or nile crepe de Chine owes its distinction to the deep scalloped V-yoke. Sizes, 14, 15, 16, $5.75

48S141   A simple step-in chemise of flesh or nile crepe de Chine has front tucks and picoted ruffle bottom. Sizes, 34 to 40, $3.50

48S142   Shaped side sections, scalloped and bound at the bottom, are the feature of this crepe de Chine step-in chemise trimmed with embroidery motif and hemstitching. Maize or peach. 34 to 38, $3.25

48S143   These bloomers in the popular shorty model are made of flesh coloured crepe de Chine with shaped front yoke and elastic back. Embroidered by hand in pastel colours. Lengths, 19 and 21 ins., $4.95

48S144   Margot pattern lace, with an interesting tab effect edge, makes the front yoke of this becoming crepe de Chine gown and edging finishes the neck and armhole. Flesh or peach. Sizes, 14, 15, 16, $4.25

48S145   This appealing georgette crepe step-in chemise has deep sections of embroidered net lace on the bottom as well as a narrow band around the top. Peach or sweet pea. Sizes, 34 to 40, $5.75

48S146   This unusual undergarment combines slip and step-in, reducing one's lingerie to the minimum. Made in pink, white or nile crepe de Chine and trimmed with Alencon pattern lace. Sizes, 34 to 40, $8.75

48S147   This crepe de Chine pyjama suit has plain coloured trousers and printed coat in harmonizing shades, attractively banded at the diagonal neckline. Green or blue. Sizes, 36 to 40, $14.75

48S148   Georgette and crepe de Chine, joined with hand-fagoting, are used for a step-in chemise of originality and charm. The bottom ruffle has a picoted edge. In peach or maize. Sizes, 34 to 40, $4.95

48S149   This handmade Porto Rican gown of flesh coloured crepe de Chine is beautifully embroidered in orchid or blue. Scalloped bottom; neck and armholes are bound. Sizes, 15, 16, 17, $7.50

48S150   Lace applique and embroidery make an attractive decoration on the front of this crepe de Chine gown with side tucks. The bottom has picoted scallops. Light blue or flesh. Sizes, 14, 15, 16, 17, $7.50

48S140
$5.75

48S142
$3.25

48S143
$4.95

48S141
$3.50

48S146
$8.75

48S148
$4.95

48S145
$5.75

48S144
$4.25

48S149
$7.50

48S147
$14.75

48S150
$7.50

Togs for Active Boys

58J150 Sturdy breeches for hiking or play are made of fast colour khaki with strong reinforcements and laced knee. Sizes, 8 to 18, $1.95

58J151 This khaki sports blouse, of soft, fast colour cotton, is ideal for play. Sizes, 8 to 14, 95c. **58J151A** In white cotton broadcloth, 95c.

58J152 Washable robe for beach or traveling, of mercerized cotton in checked effect. Blue, tan or green with white bindings. Sizes, 8 to 18, $3.75

58J153 This shaker-knit sweater in slip-on model with roll collar is an outstanding value for vacation wear. Navy only. Sizes, 8 to 18, $4.75

58J154 This two-piece all-worsted bathing suit has navy trunks and a white top. Sizes, 8 to 18, $2.95. **58J154A** One-piece style, 4 to 10, $2.25. **58J154B** White cotton webbing belt, 50c.

58J155 Trench coat of putty-coloured cotton gabardine, waterproofed and lined with plaid. Very swanky in wet weather; 8 to 18, $7.95

58J156 This marine suit of sturdy cotton cloth has a pair of white and a pair of blue shorts with white regulation middy, with blue collar and cuffs. Emblem on sleeve. Sizes, 4 to 9, $2.95

58J157 A special value is offered in this sports suit of good quality linen, in a brand-new model. White, trimmed with bindings of red or blue; or blue trimmed with white. Sizes, 4 to 9, $2.50

58J158 These separate shorts for Junior come in tan, blue, grey or white linen with self belt. Sizes, 4 to 10, $1.25

58J159 Button-on waist of durable fast-colour khaki cotton cloth; also in white; have short sleeves and sports neck. Sizes, 4 to 10, 95c.

58J160 Junior dress suit of brown, blue or green cotton broadcloth, or fast-colour khaki with self belt and short sleeves. Sizes, 3 to 9, $1.95

58J161 Boys' linen knickers, cut on men's lines, have fitted waist and side pockets. Smart designs in blues, tans or white. Sizes, 8 to 18, $1.95

58J162 An excellent tennis shirt of white, tan or blue broadcloth in regulation collar-attached style. Sizes, 12 to 14½. Specially priced, $1.50

58J163 Boys' belts in tan or black with harness buckle. Sizes, 26 to 30, $1.00

58J164 Boys' neckties in gay colours and assorted stripings, 50c.

58J165 This Junior two-trouser suit of white cotton drill in button-on style has blue collar, cuffs and belt with extra pair of blue trousers to match collar and cuffs. Sizes, 3 to 9, $2.95

58J166 A sport cap to match raincoat No. 58J155. Sizes, 6⅜ to 7⅛, $1.95

25J146 Children's cotton golf stockings in a smart variety of colour combinations. Seven-eighths length, sizes, 7 to 10½. Pair, 50c. **25J146A** Plain leg and fancy cuff, pair, 50c.

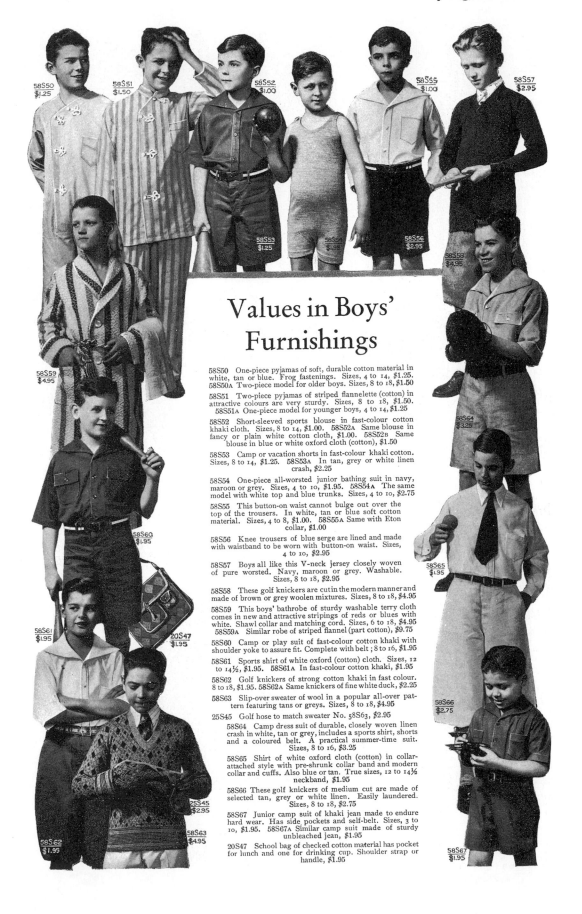

Values in Boys' Furnishings

58S50 One-piece pyjamas of soft, durable cotton material in white, tan or blue. Frog fastenings. Sizes, 4 to 14, $1.25.
58S50A Two-piece model for older boys. Sizes, 8 to 18, $1.50.

58S51 Two-piece pyjamas of striped flannelette (cotton) in attractive colours are very sturdy. Sizes, 8 to 18, $1.50.
58S51A One-piece model for younger boys, 4 to 14, $1.25

58S52 Short-sleeved sports blouse in fast-colour cotton khaki cloth. Sizes, 8 to 14, $1.00. **58S52A** Same blouse in fancy or plain white cotton cloth, $1.00. **58S52B** Same blouse in blue or white oxford cloth (cotton), $1.50

58S53 Camp or vacation shorts in fast-colour khaki cotton. Sizes, 8 to 14, $1.25. **58S53A** In tan, grey or white linen crash, $2.25

58S54 One-piece all-worsted junior bathing suit in navy, maroon or grey. Sizes, 4 to 10, $1.95. **58S54A** The same model with white top and blue trunks. Sizes, 4 to 10, $2.75

58S55 This button-on waist cannot bulge out over the top of the trousers. In white, tan or blue soft cotton material. Sizes, 4 to 8, $1.00. **58S55A** Same with Eton collar, $1.00.

58S56 Knee trousers of blue serge are lined and made with waistband to be worn with button-on waist. Sizes, 4 to 10, $2.95

58S57 Boys all like this V-neck jersey closely woven of pure worsted. Navy, maroon or grey. Washable. Sizes, 8 to 18, $2.95

58S58 These golf knickers are cut in the modern manner and made of brown or grey woolen mixtures. Sizes, 8 to 18, $4.95

58S59 This boys' bathrobe of sturdy washable terry cloth comes in new and attractive stripings of reds or blues with white. Shawl collar and matching cord. Sizes, 6 to 18, $4.95
58S59A Similar robe of striped flannel (part cotton), $9.75

58S60 Camp or play suit of fast-colour cotton khaki with shoulder yoke to assure fit. Complete with belt; 8 to 16, $1.95

58S61 Sports shirt of white oxford (cotton) cloth. Sizes, 12 to 14½, $1.95. **58S61A** In fast-colour cotton khaki, $1.95

58S62 Golf knickers of strong cotton khaki in fast colour. 8 to 18, $1.95. **58S62A** Same knickers of fine white duck, $2.25

58S63 Slip-over sweater of wool in a popular all-over pattern featuring tans or greys. Sizes, 8 to 18, $4.95

25S45 Golf hose to match sweater No. 58S63, $2.95

58S64 Camp dress suit of durable, closely woven linen crash in white, tan or grey, includes a sports shirt, shorts and a coloured belt. A practical summer-time suit. Sizes, 8 to 16, $3.25

58S65 Shirt of white oxford cloth (cotton) in collar-attached style with pre-shrunk collar band and modern collar and cuffs. Also blue or tan. True sizes, 12 to 14½ neckband, $1.95

58S66 These golf knickers of medium cut are made of selected tan, grey or white linen. Easily laundered. Sizes, 8 to 18, $2.75

58S67 Junior camp suit of khaki jean made to endure hard wear. Has side pockets and self-belt. Sizes, 3 to 10, $1.95. **58S67A** Similar camp suit made of sturdy unbleached jean, $1.95

20S47 School bag of checked cotton material has pocket for lunch and one for drinking cup. Shoulder strap or handle, $1.95

Until One Is Past Six

49S142   Wee shorts take the place of bloomers in a cunning little frock of copen or yellow cotton broadcloth, and smocking on each side of the small white vestee gives fulness. Sizes, 2 to 6 years, $4.75

49S143   Little brother's suit has a flowered dimity blouse with frilled front and collar to match little sister's frock No. 49S144. The button-on trousers are of blue chambray. Sizes, 2 to 4 years, $3.25

49S144   Very crisp and gay is little sister's dimity frock flowered in rose-and-blue to match little brother's suit No. 49S143. The abbreviated length reveals matching bloomers. Sizes, 2 to 6 years, $3.25

49S145   Figured percale in a quaint pattern combining gold-and-blue makes a becoming frock for a very young lady. 2 to 6 years, $2.25

49S146   Hand embroidery to delight the youthful eye trims the white dimity shirt of this young man's suit and cotton broadcloth in peach or copen makes collar, cuffs and trousers. Sizes, 2 to 4 years, $2.50

49S147   A charming frock for the little tot is made of cotton print in rose or green and has bloomers to match. Sizes, 2 to 6 years, $3.50

49S148   White dimity printed in a sprightly pattern combining red, green and yellow makes this appealing bloomer frock. 2 to 6 years, $3.90

49S149   Tangerine or green chambray makes the button-on shorts of this boys' suit and trims the printed dimity blouse. 2 to 4 years, $2.25

49S150   This little miss is very demure in her cotton broadcloth dress with matching bloomers. Blue or apricot. Sizes, 2 to 6 years, $3.90

49S151   Very self-important is this youngster in a suit of cotton Devonshire cloth with mannish self-belt. Cuffs, collar and triangular pockets are contrastingly piped. Yellow or lavender. Sizes, 2 to 5 years, $3.90

49S152   Cross-stitching trims the coat of this small boys' suit of linen in copen or lavender. White collar and cuffs. Sizes, 2 to 4 years, $3.90

49S153   Hand-buttonholed cut-outs trim this little boys' smart suit of copen or yellow cotton broadcloth. Sizes, 2 to 4 years, $2.75

49S154   Printed cotton material in either rose or copen makes this dainty little frock for the small girl. Sizes, 1 to 3 years, $1.75

When One Is Very Young

49S157 A delightful frock for the tiny miss is made of peach or lavender linen to match brother's suit No. 49S158. White linen vestee, collar, cuffs and pockets increase its charm. Sizes, 2 to 6 years, $5.50

49S158 Made to match sister's frock No. 49S157, this little boys' suit of peach or lavender linen also has a white linen vestee, collar and cuffs. The tiny shorts button to the blouse. Sizes, 2 to 5 years, $5.50

49S159 Figured batiste in combinations of red-and-blue or blue-and-yellow on a white ground makes a charming frock for any child from 1 to 3 years, $1.25

49S160 Pointed smocking at the shoulders and white collar and cuffs with hand-crocheted lace trim a smart little frock made of imported dotted Swiss in all-white, pink or yellow. Sizes, 2 to 6 years, $7.50

49S161 Little boys' suit of copen or yellow linen, smartly finished with collar and cuffs with embroidered dots. Sizes, 2 to 4 years, $3.25

49S162 The small girl will be very gay in this attractive little frock of printed lawn with its pointed collar and cuffs of white organdie. Blue-and-pink print on a white ground. Sizes, 2 to 6 years, $2.10

49S163 A "dressed-up" little suit for a very young man is made of linen and trimmed with hand-crocheted lace on the collar and cuffs. Comes in all-white, yellow or lavender. Sizes, 2 to 4 years, $4.75

49S164 A figured batiste frock with collar and cuffs of lavender and a triangular pocket; has matching bloomers. Sizes, 2 to 6 years, $3.25

49S165 A bloomer dress of figured percale in blue or lavender is a practical choice for the small daughter. Sizes, 2 to 6 years, $3.25

49S166 A striped cotton broadcloth combining peach and green makes a child's frock that is distinctly "different." Sizes, 2 to 6 years, $4.75

49S167 A hand-embroidered pocket is the swanky touch on this young man's suit of copen or yellow chambray. Pique collar. 2 to 4 years, $2.25

49S168 Very "collegiate" indeed is this youngster's suit of white cotton-shorts buttoned on to a blouse of bright-coloured cotton print with large pearl buttons. Comes in sizes 2 to 5 years, $3.25

49S169 This bloomer dress of copen or lavender cotton broadcloth buttons smartly over a panel of white material. Sizes, 2 to 6 years, $4.75

New for Junior

58F55 $4.95

58F56 $4.95

58F69 $1.00 Blouse

58F71 50¢ Tie

58F68 $4.95

58F70 $2.95 Shorts

58F72 50¢ Belt

58F73 $7.50

58F75 $2.95

58F76 $5.50

58F74 $4.00 Trousers

58F77 $1.00 Shirt

58F79 50¢ Tie

58F80 50¢ Belt

58F78 $2.50 Shorts

58F81 $5.50

58F82 $3.95

58F83 $2.95

58F57 $15.00

58F59 $2.00 Cap.

58F58 $10.50 Suit

58F60 $13.50 Coat

58F61 $2.50 Cap.

58F64 $2.50 Cap

58F62 $16.50 Coat

58F63 $2.95 Suit

58F67 $2.50 Cap.

58F65 $12.50 Coat

58F66 $12.50 Suit.

58F84 $1.50

58F85 $1.00

39F60 $5.50

58F55 Suit with hairline shirting blouse and tweed trousers. Mannish collar and silk tie. Tan with brown shorts, blue with black and white. Sizes, 4 to 9, $4.95.

58F56 *Regulation suit of white galatea with navy serge collar, cuffs and shorts. Emblem on sleeve, and black silk tie. Sizes, 4 to 9, $4.95. 58F56A Same as No. 58F56 in two-piece middy style. 4 to 10, $4.95*

58F57 Double-breasted ulster overcoat in grey or brown herringbone, wool lined. Sizes, 4 to 10, $15.00

58F58 *Jacket suit of herringbone cheviot in brown, grey, or in plain navy blue. Collarless model; 2 pairs shorts. Sizes, 5 to 10, $10.50*

58F59 Eaton cap of navy cloth. 6⅝ to 7⅛ inches, $2.00

58F60 *Leather jacket in brown, green, or red capeskin, wool lined. Sizes, 4 to 10, $13.50*

58F61 Helmet to match No. 58F60, $2.50

58F62 *Coat of navy Germania chinchilla, wool lining, gilt buttons and emblem on sleeve or cinnamon brown with bone buttons. Sizes, 4 to 10, $16.50*

58F63 Suit of tweed trousers with striped shirting blouse. Tan with brown, blue with grey. Sizes, 4 to 9, $2.95

58F64 *Polo hat to match No. 58F62. 6⅝ to 7⅛ inches, $2.50*

58F65 Regulation navy coat tailored in soft woolens with solid colour lining, gilt buttons and emblem on sleeves. Sizes, 4 to 10, $12.50

58F66 *Jacket suit of mannish cut in grey or brown mixtures or navy cheviot. Two pairs of shorts. Sizes, 5 to 10, $12.50*

58F67 Polo hat to match No. 58F65. 6⅝ to 7⅛ inches, $2.50

58F68 *Regulation suit of blue Palmer cloth top with navy serge collar, cuffs and shorts, emblem on sleeve, black silk tie. Sizes, 4 to 9, $4.95. 58F68A Same as No. 58F68 in two-piece middy style. 4 to 10, $4.95*

58F69 Broadcloth button-on blouse. Tan, blue, green, or white. 5 to 10, $1.00

58F70 *Tweed shorts of excellent woolens, in tan or grey. Sizes, 5 to 10, $2.95*

58F71 Junior boys' tie in solid brown, green, red or blue, 50c.

58F72 *Leather belt with buckle. Brown or black. Sizes, 26 to 30 inches, 50c.*

58F73 Navy serge regulation suit with shorts. Trimming correct in every detail. Middy style. Sizes, 4 to 10; button-on style, sizes, 4 to 9, $7.50

58F74 *Long sailor trousers to match (illustrated) No. 58F73, $4.00*

58F75 Middy suit of blue cotton with regulation trimming: white tape, red emblem and black silk tie. Button-on style, sizes, 4 to 9; middy style, sizes, 4 to 10, $2.95

58F76 *Suit with broadcloth blouse and flannel shorts. Mannish collar, silk tie and leather belt. White with grey; tan with brown, or blue with navy. Sizes, 4 to 9, $5.50*

58F77 Button-on blouse of cotton with mannish collar and neat stripings. Sizes, 5 to 10, $1.00

58F78 *Brown corduroy shorts, full lined. Sizes, 5 to 10, $2.50*

58F79 Junior boys' tie with smart stripes, 50c.

58F80 *Leather belt with buckle. Brown or black. 26 to 30 inches, 50c.*

58F81 Two-piece jersey suit with contrasting stripe on collar and cuffs. Middy style, sizes, 4 to 10; button-on, sizes, 4 to 9. Brown, green or navy, $5.50

58F82 *Suit of tan linen blouse and brown jersey shorts, or white linen with navy jersey. Leather belt and sport collar. Sizes, 4 to 9, $3.95*

58F83 Suit with brown striped shirting blouse and brown corduroy shorts or blue stripe with blue shorts. Sport collar. Sizes, 4 to 9, $2.95

58F84 *Pajamas similar to No. 58F85, two-piece style. Sizes, 8 to 18, $1.50*

58F85 Domet cotton flannel pajamas, one-piece style with stripings. Sizes, 6 to 14, $1.00

39F60 *Sturdy school oxfords made of tan Norwegian grain leather and built on a combination last which assures a snug fitting at the heel. Leather soles and heels. Widths, B to E, sizes, 1 to 6. Widths, A to E, sizes, 4 to 6, $5.50. 39F60A May also be had in black calfskin, $5.50*

and Big Brother

58F92
$1.50 Cap.

58F93
$1.95 Shirt

58F94
$1.00 Tie

58F90
$6.00
Sweater

58F91
$3.00 Knickers

58F96
$12.50 Coat

58F95
$6.75
Knickers

58F98
$1.95
Helmet

58F97
$7.95 Coat

58F100
$4.50 Hat

58F99
$20.00 Coat

58F101
$10.75
Coat

58F102
$4.75
Knickers

58F103
$20.00

58F104
$14.50

58F106
$28.50

58F105
$19.50

58F110
$1.95
Shirt

58F111
75¢
Tie

58F109
$2.95

58F108
$14.50

58F107
$28.50

58F112
$3.50

58F114
$8.50

58F116
$2.95
Helmet

58F113
$4.95

58F119
$1.00 Hat

58F120
$7.50
Set

58F122
$8.50 Set

58F123
$4.75

58F122

58F115
$15.50

58F117
$6.50

58F118
$4.75

58F121
$4.00

58F120

58F90 Shaker knit, slip-on heavy sweater, with roll collar. In navy, maroon
or grey. Sizes, 28 to 36, $6.00

58F91 *Brown corduroy knickers of sturdy construction, full cut, and lined throughout. Sizes, 8 to 18, $3.00*

58F92 Knitted skating cap in navy, maroon or grey, $1.50

58F93 *Collar-attached shirt of good quality oxford cloth, in tan, green, blue or
white. Sizes, 12 to 14½ neck, $1.95*

58F94 Silk tie of plain colour. In red, green, blue or brown, $1.00

58F95 *Breeches for hiking or riding. Of good quality brown corduroy with double
seat and knee. Sizes, 8 to 18, $6.75*

58F96 Leather windbreaker, wool-lined with knitted cuffs and waistband. Roomy
and well tailored. In brown only. Sizes, 8 to 18, $12.50

58F97 *Trench coat of cotton gabardine with full plaid lining. Sizes, 8 to 18, $7.95*

58F98 Helmet to match No. 58F97. Sizes, 6⅝ to 7⅛, $1.95

58F99 *Boy's school coat, finely tailored of grey or brown wool in conservative
patterns and very good quality. Full lining of wool with Venetian yoke and sleeve
lining. Sizes, 11 to 18, $20.00*

58F100 Felt hat of good quality and approved styling. In brown or grey. Sizes,
6⅝ to 7⅛, $4.50

58F101 *Cotton moleskin sheep-lined coat with dyed lambskin collar which will
not crock. An especially favoured model. Sizes, 8 to 18, $10.75*

58F102 Knickers in navy cloth, sturdy and practical, full cut and full lined.
Sizes, 8 to 18, $4.75

58F103 *Blue cheviot suit for formal occasions. In single- or double-breasted
models, well tailored. Coat, vest and two pairs of knickers. Sizes, 8 to 16, $20.00*

58F104 Four-piece school suit of good quality herringbone cheviot in grey or brown.
Coat, vest and two pairs knickers. Sizes, 8 to 16, $14.50

58F105 *Four-piece suit of imported tweed in grey or brown mixtures. Coat, vest
and two pairs of plus-fours. Sizes, 8 to 16, $19.50*

58F106 Four-piece prep school suit. Single-breasted model with one pair of long
and one pair golf trousers. Tailored of strong woolen fabric in neat grey or brown
herringbone patterns. Sizes, 15 to 20, $28.50

58F107 *Prep suit of good quality navy blue cloth for dress
occasions. In single- or double-brested models with two
pairs of long trousers, coat and vest. Finely tailored.
Sizes, 15 to 20, $28.50*

58F108 School suit of dark brown corduroy, a staunch
ally. Cut full and lined throughout. Single-breasted coat,
vest and two pairs of knickers. Sizes, 8 to 16, $14.50

58F109 *Knitted jersey, slip-over model of all-worsted
with V-neck. In navy, grey or maroon. 28 to 36, $2.95*

58F110 Collar attached broadcloth shirt in white, tan,
blue or green. 12 to 14½ neck, $1.95

58F111 *Tie in attractive stripings, 75c.*

58F112 Sturdy tweed knickers in grey or brown, full
lined. Sizes, 8 to 18, $3.50

58F113 *Blanket robe in attractive and colourful designs.
Full cut shawl collar. Well tailored. Sizes, 8 to 18, $4.95*

58F114 Flannel robe in bright coloured stripes. Good
quality all-wool cloth. Sizes, 8 to 18, $8.50

58F115 *Horsehide leather coat in dark mahogany colour,
full lined with wool plaid. Unusually sturdy construction.
Sizes, 8 to 18, $15.50*

58F116 Leather helmet, suede cloth lined. Sizes, 6⅝
to 7⅛, $2.95

58F117 *Plus-four knickers well tailored of fine quality
wool in grey or brown. Sizes, 10 to 18, $6.50*

58F118 Yellow oilskin slicker. Sizes, 8 to 18, $4.75

58F119 *Sou-wester to match No. 58F118. 6⅝ to 7⅛, $1.00*

58F120 Wool sweater and hose set of tan, blue or green all-
over pattern, plain hose with matching cuffs. 28 to 36, $7.50

58F121 *Fine quality brown corduroy knickers, full lined
and well cut. Sizes, 8 to 18, $4.00*

58F122 Novelty polo wool sweater and sports hose set. In
heather mixtures with polo player design. In tan, blue
or maroon. Sizes, 28 to 36, $8.50

58F123 *Tweed knickers in tan or grey mixtures. Full
cut. Sizes, 8 to 18, $4.75*

45F51 Uplift bandeau of sturdy pink silk, cut low at back, with elastic insert. Ribbon shoulder straps. Sizes, 32 to 38, 95c.

45F52 *Side-hook girdle of lined pink moire, a boneless model with side sections of elastic, and two pairs of supporters attached. Sizes, 26 to 32, $3.50*

45F53 Semi-step-in model of rose crepe ninon elaborately lace-trimmed with surgical elastic sections and front gore. A supple model utterly free of boning. Two pairs of supporters attached. Sizes, 26 to 32, $6.75

45F54 *Shaped uplift bandeau of lace with pink stitching, unusual in design and very attractive. Has elastic insert at back. Sizes, 32 to 38, $2.00*

45F55 Foundation with inner boned belt for abdominal support is made of firm pink broche with elastic side sections and front gore. Boned lengthwise in back and horizontally over the outer front section. Three pairs of supporters attached. To be ordered according to bust measure for sizes, 34 to 44, $5.00

45F56 *Side-hook corset of pink broche with side sections and front gore of surgical elastic. Boned front and back. Three pairs of supporters attached. Sizes, 28 to 38, $7.75*

45F57 Uplift bandeau of pink milanese with supporting band and back of matching tricot. Elastic inserts at front and back. Sizes, 32 to 40, $1.50

45F58 *Fasso step-in, made in Paris, of rose surgical elastic finely woven and fashioned in front for comfort. A delicate design is woven in the top. Three pairs of supporters attached. Sizes, 26 to 34, $6.75*

45F59 Imported bandeau of fine lace lined and edged with flesh coloured net and daintily trimmed with ribbon buds. Narrow elastic insert at back which is low. Sizes, 30 to 36, $2.00

45F60 *Fasso step-in, made in Paris for Altman, of rose surgical elastic fashioned at front and boned lightly at front. Short lacing at waistline in back assures comfortable fitting. Three pairs of supporters attached. Sizes, 28 to 34, $10.00*

45F61 Imported evening uplift bandeau of fine lace and satin. Has ribbon covered elastic crossing at back which buttons on front shield. Ribbon shoulder straps and bud trimming. Sizes, 32 to 36, $3.50

45F62 *For the princesse silhouette this semi-step-in foundation made of imported figured batiste with surgical elastic inserts is ideally fitted to assume its fashion responsibility for autumn. Uplift is made of fine lace, net lined, and garment is cut low at back. Lightly boned at the back. Three pairs of supporters attached. To be ordered according to bust measure. 34 to 44, $10.00*

45F63 Foundation garment of pink broche with shaped uplift and under-arm sections of matching tricot. Elastic side sections and front gore. Boned front and back with an inner band over abdomen. Two pairs of supporters attached. To be ordered according to bust measure. Sizes, 34 to 44, $5.00

46F85 *Knitted rayon pajamas—a charming two-piece model which uses an effective contrast of a deeper tone. In beige or nile. Sizes, 15, 16, 17, $3.95*

46F86 Betalph milanese silk pantie in flesh or peach colour with very pretty lace trimming in bow-knot design. Sizes, 5, 6, 7, $2.95

46F87 *Vest to match pantie No. 46F86. Sizes, 34 to 40, $2.25*

46F88 Betalph milanese silk bloomer in peach colour with deep-toned ecru lace insert. Size, 5, 6, 7, $3.50

46F89 *Vest to match pantie No. 46F88. Sizes, 36 to 42, $2.50*

46F90 Betalph milanese silk banded pantie with embroidered motif and applique. In flesh colour with contrasting band and applique. Sizes, 5, 6, 7, $2.95

46F91 *Vest to match pantie No. 46F90. Sizes, 36 to 42, $2.75*

46F92 Betalph milanese silk pantie of flesh or nile colour with striking applique design in a deeper tone. Sizes, 5, 6, 7, $2.95

46F93 *Vest to match pantie No. 46F92. Sizes, 36 to 42, $2.25*

46F94 Betalph Milanese silk gown of flesh or peach colour with deep lace insertion of exquisite design at the neck, and net edge at the botton. Sizes, 15, 16, 17, $5.75

46F95 *Betalph pure glove silk bloomers in plain tailored flesh colour. Sizes, 5, 6, 7, $2.10*

46F96 Plain tailored vest to match pantie No. 46F95. 34 to 42, $1.55

Hand Embroidered Daintiness

47F30 Nightgown of excellent quality white nainsook, slip-over model forming a V-front, trimmed with Val. lace and embroidery, set-in sleeve. Sizes, 14, 15, 16, 17, $2.95

47F31 *White cambric nightgown with long sleeves, yoke of insertion embroidery and cluster tucking, embroidery ruffle on neck and sleeves. Sizes, 14, 15, 16, 17, $1.95. Size, 18, $2.75*

47F32 Tuck-in pajama of large checked print trimmed with solid colour yoke on neck and trousers. Sizes, 36 and 40. Colours, blue or orange, $1.95

47F33 *Slip-over pajama of novelty flannelette with pink or blue ground trimmed with white. Trousers of white trimmed to match long-sleeved coat. Sizes, 36 and 40, $1.95*

47F34 Surplice pajama of cotton broadcloth in tri-coloured coin-dot design on white ground. Coat ties on one side. Sizes, 36 and 40. Colours in varied assortments, $1.95

47F35 *Stripe flannelette pajama with collar vestee of plain colour trimmed with matching novelty braid. Assorted stripes. Sizes, 36 and 40, $2.75*

47F36 White nainsook slip-over nightgown with elbow sleeves trimmed with embroidery insertion and edge, ribbon run. Sizes, 14, 15, 16, 17, $1.95. Size, 18, $2.75

47F37 *Nightgown of solid colour flannelette, pajama effect, frog trimmed. In pink or blue. Sizes, 15, 16, 17, $1.50*

Warmth for Zero Weather

47F38 Nightgown of striped flannelette with yoke neck. Sizes, 15, 16, 17, $1.95. Size, 18, $2.75

47F39 *Flannelette pajama with frog-trimmed coat, blazer stripes. Sizes, 36, and 40, $1.95*

47F40 Nightgown of striped flannelette, slip-over model with collar and vestee bound with satin ribbon. Feather-stitched trimming. Sizes, 15, 16, 17, $1.95. Size, 18, $2.75

47F41 *Philippine handmade nightgown of white nainsook hand embroidered, sleeveless. Patterns may vary. Sizes, 15, 16, 17, $1.95*

47F42 Step-in chemise handmade in Porto Rico of white nainsook with appliques, embroidery and binding in colour. Designs may vary. 36 to 44, $1.50

47F43 *White nainsook costume slip with built-up shoulder, filet lace trimmed, hemstitching in front and shadow hem. Sizes, 36, 38, 40, 42, 44, $1.95*

47F44 Pantie of novelty print on white ground, yoke band and elastic back. Lengths, 17 or 19 inches, 95c.

47F45 *Philippine handmade nightgown of white nainsook with kimono sleeve, hand embroidered. Designs may vary. Sizes, 15, 16, 17, $1.50*

47F46 Fine quality white nainsook gown with long sleeve. Trimmed with imitation point de Paris lace, cluster tucking and featherstitching. Button front. Sizes, 14, 15, 16, 17, $2.95

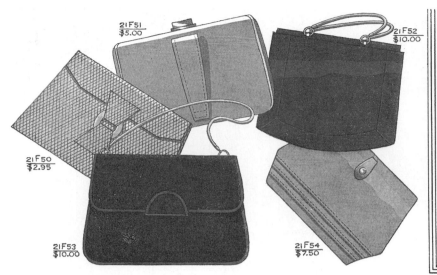

21F50   Envelope purse with flap on each side in diced grain leather. Large center pocket is fitted with purse and mirror. In black, brown, tan or navy, $2.95

21F51   *Flat pouch purse with backstrap and inside frame compartment. In red, green, tan, brown, navy, or black calfskin, $5.00*

21F52   Tailored purse has inverted clasp, inside frame purse and novel snake chain metal handles. Black, brown, navy or dark green calf; or in black or brown suede, $10.00

21F53   *Soft pouch bag with snake chain handle that slips through flap which has a tab fastening. Large extra pocket inside, frame purse and large mirror attached. In black or brown suede; or in black, brown, or navy calfskin, $10.00*

21F54   Neatly tailored backstrap purse of calfskin with corded bottom, metal lift lock and inside frame purse. In black, tan, navy or brown, $7.50

21F55   *Very attractive metal beaded evening bag in gold and silver colourings on metal frame with chain. Designs may vary, $2.95*

21F56   Imitation pearl beads and vari-coloured embroidery are used in this flat envelope which may be worn without chain, $5.00

21F57   *A favourite for evening is this bag of imitation pearl and glass beads intricately designed and mounted with a plain silver-finished frame, or suntan beads on a gilt-finished frame, $7.50*

21F58   Large, vagabond calf pouch in two-tone colourings with large cuter pocket and metal fastening. Inner section has a secure pocket with chain fastening and is fitted with purse and mirror. In tan-and-brown, brown-and-tan, all-black, dark green with light green, navy with lighter blue, $7.50

21F59   *Calfskin semi-pouch with chain fastening at top has a backstrap and novel metal ornament. In black, brown, navy or green, $5.00*

21F60   Large, soft envelope of calfskin with deep outer pocket and leather-cord handle. Inside, which is very deep and roomy, has a pocket full size and coin purse attached to lining bound with matching leather. Also fitted with mirror. In black, brown, navy or bottle green, $12.50

21F61   *Pouch bag of lizard grain leather with inside frame compartment. In black, tan, navy, brown or green, $2.95*

21F62   Strap purse of suede with genuine lizard trim. Amply secure with its envelope flap which covers a sturdy frame. Inside frame purse and mirror, nicely lined and fitted. In black or brown, $7.50

21F63   *Calfskin strap purse with concealed frame and clasp is mounted with a decorative enamel plaque in colour. Inside frame compartment and mirror. In black, tan or navy calf; or in black or brown suede, $7.50*

21F64   Calfskin pouch bag with triple frame which provides two completely separated inner compartments, fitted with purse and mirror. In black, tan or brown, $5.00

21F65   *Tailored calfskin envelope of the sort that is indispensable for business or travel because of the several pockets and compartments and double inside frame. Has a strap back and neat metal ornament. Very nicely finished and compact. In tan, brown, or black, $10.00*

21F66   Swagger pouch bag of suede with chain fastening at the top and double handles joined to square metal links at both sides. Inside frame purse and mirror. Available in black or brown suede; or in black, tan or navy calf, $5.00

Many other fashionable styles are offered by the Hand Bag Department—First Floor

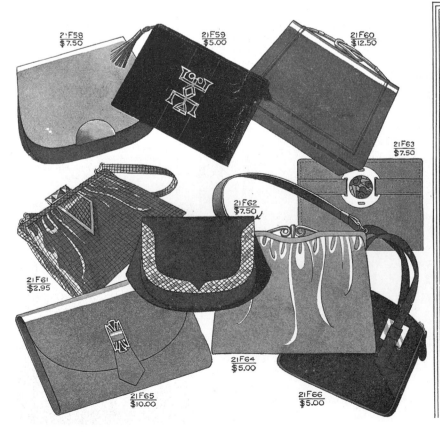

Footsteps Are in Graceful
Line from Heel to Toe

Balta Shoes

Balta shoes, exclusive with B. Altman & Co., are made to conform to the highest standards of footwear construction

These are but a few of the many smart new models shown in our

SHOE SALON—SECOND FLOOR

53F60 A splendid addition to the afternoon costume—this classic one-strap model with neat center buckle. Black suede with silver piping, or brown suede with gold. Black lizard vamp with patent leather quarter, or brown lizard vamp with brown kid quarter, $12.50

Sizes, 3½ to 7½, in B and C widths

53F61 *Fashion highlights no smarter model than this one of plain crepe de Chine in black or white which may be dyed any shade to match sample without extra charge, $12.50*

Sizes, 5 to 7½, in AA and A widths

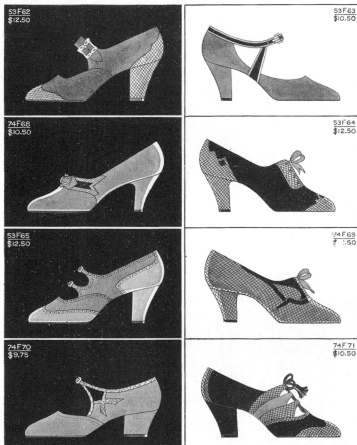

53F62 *A widely favoured model with Cuban heel and broad strap. Brown or black suede are the leathers used, and these are trimmed with self coloured genuine lizard, $12.50*

74F68 Supremely qualified for college entrance is this step-in pump of black, blue or brown suede with self-colour trim of genuine lizard, and black patent or brown kid with beige lizard, $10.50

53F65 *Unusually smart lines appear in this tailleur twin-strap model of suede and calf in brown or black, $12.50*

74F70 A low heel, one-strap model with well rounded toe, available in black or brown suede with matching trim of real alligator, $9.75

53F63 A dignified and modern touch is given to this afternoon slipper in its novel treatment of straps in two-tone kid. Black, brown, or blue suede, or black patent, $10.50

53F64 *Distinctive because of its unique design is this Cuban heel oxford in black, brown or blue suede with self trim of genuine lizard, $12.50*

74F69 Exceptional value is obtained in this oxford of genuine lizard, highly fashionable and immensely practical. In black or brown with matching trim of kid, or in blue lizard with astrolac trim, $12.50

74F71 *An Autumn perennial that varies its appearance slightly with smart trim of combined leathers. In black suede with black lizard and patent leather trim, or brown suede with brown lizard and kid trim, $10.50*

74F72 *Deft manipulation of leather forms an interesting design on this striking model of blue kid and suede, brown kid and suede, black patent with gunmetal silk kid, $10.50*

53F66 The opera pump—suitable for all types of costumes and widely acclaimed when made on the Balta last, which fits the narrow heel. Regent opera shown in black lizard with black mat kid quarter, brown lizard with brown kid, blue lizard with blue kid, $12.50

53F67 The high instep may snuggle contentedly into this oxford with well-fitting arch. Black mat kid vamp with black suede quarter, brown kid with brown suede, or blue kid with blue suede, $10.50

74F73 *To complete the cycle of suitability this all-lizard one-strap is offered in black, brown or blue colourings with dainty trim of matching kid and inlay of lighter lizard, $12.50*

Frocks That Flare and Fall in the Newest Manner

The selection of your complete wardrobe, in our Magazine Section, Sixth Floor, will make shopping delightfully simple. Coats, smart accessories, frocks, hats— in fact most of the merchandise shown in the magazine is assembled here for your convenience

33F63 One-piece tailored frock of novelty checked silk-and-wool eminently suited for travel wear. A beige crepe vestee with contrasting silk tie and novelty buttons lend youthful interest. A wide fold of the material forms the hipband with novel closing, one end crossed through a buttonhole slit. Skirt is box-plaited all around. Brown with brown tie, or navy with red tie. Sizes, 14 to 20, $16.75

33F64 An afternoon dress of canton crepe and matching transparent velvet with horizontal tucking which is so new and flattering. Two full flared tiers banded with velvet form the skirt, which is worn a little longer to conform with the latest Paris advices regarding hemlines. In black, cedar green or Independence blue. 14 to 20, $19.75

33F60 Two-piece georgette model with transparent velvet trim, a row of ornamental buttons and plaited ecru lace frill. The skirt with double side plaits all around is attached to a full length foundation of crepe de Chine with built-up shoulders. The front horizontal tucking is a note which appears on many exceedingly smart fall gowns. Blouse fits snugly at the hips by means of inverted seam plaiting. Colours, chocolate brown, claret red, black or Independence blue. Sizes, 14 to 20, $19.75

33F61 *Simulated two-piece gown of brocaded velvet. A circular skirt with irregular hemline lends daytime formality which is further accented by dressmaker details appearing in the shirred hipband and the flattering shoulder trim of contrasting georgette bows and streamers. The blouse and skirt are both attached to a silk crepe foundation. In black, brown or copen blue. Sizes, 14 to 20; 38 and 40, $19.75*

33F62 A splendid gown for mature figures. Every detail describes its suitability and fashion-rightness. A one-piece model of canton crepe with pleasing accents of matching transparent velvet. A hipband with narrow tucking assures snug-fitting and a graceful contour. The long, narrow scalloped collar is designed to give height. In black, navy or chestnut brown. In sizes, 38½, 40½, 42½, 44½, 46½, 48½, $16.75

33F65 *One-piece coat dress of silk mixture in a checked travel print. An inserted panel of side plaits extends from the shoulders in the center back to the hem giving fulness and striking variety in design. The diagonal influence is seen at the skirt closing where a plaited section is joined. Novelty buttons, bound buttonholes, notched collar with surplice revers, self-belt in back and contrasting silk crepe vestee are all fashionable details. In blue-and-brown, tan-and-red, beige-and-green, grey-and-blue. Sizes, 36 to 46, $16.75*

33F59 One-piece model of self bordered silk-and-wool novelty crepe. Hipband and bow ties are fashioned of the print while the neck yoke and hem adopt the border. The skirt is group plaited all around. A conservative model for the long journey, or wherever extra wear is required. In black-and-eggshell or blue-and-grey. Sizes, 36 to 46, $19.75

The "Extra Frock" Department Provides Added Smartness—Inexpensively

From the Magazine Section, Sixth Floor. See page 23 for additional frocks at $16.75 and $19.75 from this section.

33F56 One-piece canton crepe frock with surplice blouse and youthful scarf. Contrasting georgette vest and double jabot are fastened by novelty pin. Cluster of plaits at side finish the tunic effect which fastens at the hip with an adjustable tie. Black with flesh, English green with eggshell, brown with beige. Sizes, 16 and 18; 38 to 46, $16.75

33F52
$19.75

33F53
$19.75

33F54
$16.75

33F55
$19.75

33F56
$16.75

33F58
$16.75

33F57
$19.75

33F52 Two-piece tailored covert frock. Youthful V-neck ends in novelty opening fastened by pert tabs. Bands at the wrist of beige crepe are repeated in the vestee attached to skirt bodice and hand embroidered. Beige crepe scalloped collar in back. The skirt has a flared front achieved by circular unpressed box-plaits and is given additional fulness by side-plaits in the back. Red, green, blue. Sizes, 16 to 20; 38 to 42, $19.75

33F53 *Three-piece suit, wool tweed skirt and finger-tip jacket. Skirt with group of side-plaits is attached to a bodice. Smart motif of the tweed at neck of blouse. The well-fitted tailored coat has a turn-back collar and patch pockets. Selvage trim finishes the cuffs, pockets and front. Brown mixture with natural long-sleeved jersey blouse, black and white mixture with grey blouse. Sizes, 14 to 18; 38 and 40, $19.75*

33F54 This one-piece canton crepe frock has a charming side V-neck trimmed with narrow lace. Smartly fitted hipband is trimmed by novelty pin. Two narrow circular tiers, one of matching transparent velvet and one of the canton crepe, are draped over the circular skirt. Velvet bow at neck and velvet cuffs. Black, hunter green, Independence blue. Sizes, 14 to 20, $16.75

33F55 *One-piece dress of satin features a flattering two-toned side drape on blouse to match the tabs at the bottom of the raglan sleeves and the trimming on the V-neck. Two bands of self-fabric forming a fitted hipband end in flare at side of skirt which is open to form a wrap-around. Black with flesh, brown with beige. Sizes, 16 and 18; 38 to 44, $19.75*

33F57 One-piece dress of novelty wool mixture. Notched collar forms a V-neck. Bands of self material down the front and back top the all-around novelty plaited skirt. Green or light brown. Sizes, 14 to 18; 38 and 40, $19.75

33F58 *One-piece canton crepe frock has a diagonal line at front of blouse which continues across back and forms the upper line of the fitted hipband. Circular skirt has flared fulness at both sides. Matching transparent velvet bows and trimming. Black, chocolate brown, wine red. Sizes, 14 to 20, $16.75*

Costumes for Town and Country

From the Sports Department

8F81 A raincoat of rubberized silvertone jersey lined with plaid is a trusty protection in stormy weather. Desert brown, pine green, or oxford. Sizes, 14 to 18; 38 to 44, $7.50

8F82 *A tweed coat dress with harmonizing bengaline vestee and collar. Side pockets, leather lined tweed belt and bright metal buttons. Lavender or oxford with grey vestee or green with beige. 16 and 18; 38 to 44, $25.00*

8F83 This youthful three-piece diagonal mousse ensemble with long-sleeved beige silk crepe blouse will be a great favourite for college campus or wear about town. Jacket has set-in panels ending in a pocket at each side. Belt from side seam fastens at front with smart buckle. Skirt on yoke has cluster of plaits at front and is belted so that blouse may be worn tuck-in fashion or as an overblouse. Seal brown or navy. Sizes, 14 to 20, $39.50

8F84 *A particularly attractive version of the peasant dress that is always in favour. Charmingly hand-smocked at waist, neck and cuffs in two harmonizing tones to match the hand embroidery and hand fagoting on the sleeves. Meadow-green, royal blue, chestnut brown flat crepe. Sizes, 14 to 20. May be specially ordered in size 40, $19.75*

8F85 Snug and comfortable is this camel's hair coat of novelty weave. The collar makes an attractive frame for the face. Unique cuffs are trimmed with buttons. Matching crepe lining and warm interlining. Acorn brown with raccoon or squirrel grey with grey wolf. Sizes, 16 and 18; 38 to 44, $59.50

8F86 *The contrasting tie, buttons and monogram of this two-piece canton crepe frock are charmingly youthful. The skirt is novelty plaited all around to a silk crepe bodice top. Imperial blue with red trim, Madeira wine with black, Kaffa brown with brown. Sizes, 14 to 20, $19.75*

8F87 Beautifully tailored dress of canton crepe. The skirt is finely plaited all around and is stitched just below the belt for a snug hipline. Blouse is finished with bone buttons to match the buckle on the stitched self belt. Detachable crepe collar and cuffs. Larkspur blue with white. Burgoyne red with white. Kaffa brown with beige. Sizes, 14 to 18; 38 and 40, $19.75

34F43 *Hat described on page 11*

34F47 *A Descat copy of felt with cut brim which folds back and forms a long streamer end. This is slipped through a slit in the crown and drawn into a flat bow. In new red or sand, $10.00*

34F48 A new model in Agnes' own inimitable style. Fitted turban with scalloped brim and leaf-shaped end which hugs the cheek. Metal ornament at the side. In beige or black soleil, $7.50

34F52 A velvet cloche after Descat with slightly rippled brim and grosgrain ribbon band. In seal brown or black, $7.50

34F41, 34F44, 34F46 Hats described on pages 5 and 22

21F70 *Envelope of calfskin with leather piping in pleasing contrast. Large inside envelope of lining material and mirror. In black, tan, brown, navy or green, $5.00*

21F71 Envelope of couturier design with points piped in harmonizing leather. Nicely lined and fitted with purse and mirror. In black, brown, navy or dark green calfskin; or in black or brown suede, $10.00

21F72 *Vagabound purse of boarded grained leather with multiple fittings consisting of mirror, powder box, lipstick, comb, purse. In blue, tan, red, black, brown or green, $2.95*

34F52 $7.50 HAT

8F81 $7.50

34F41 $12.50 Hat

8F82 $25.00 Dress

8F83 $39.50 Suit

34F46 $7.50 Hat

34F44 $5.00 Hat

8F86 Dress $19.75

8F87 $19.75

8F84 $19.75 Dress

34F47 $10.00 Hat

34F48 $7.50 Hat

8F85 $59.50 Coat

34F43 $7.50

21F70 $5.00

21F71 $10.00

21F72 $2.95

Silk and Velvet Effect Flaring Godets

70F40 Matching transparent velvet trimming gives soft charm to this canton crepe frock. The V-neck is attractively edged with contrasting satin fold. Clever treatment of the velvet jabot graciously breaks the surplice line which ends just above a tie at the wide hipband. The wrap-around skirt, banded with velvet, has a smartly irregular circular drape on one side. Burgoyne red, Philippine brown, black. Sizes, 36 to 46, $25.00

59F41 *The coat of this three-piece transparent velvet suit is effectively scalloped at the bottom, repeating the treatment at the bottom of the skirt, which is flared in a circular manner on a snug hip yoke. Buttons studded with brilliants adorn the hip opening. The sleeveless blouse is of eggshell satin, stitched in colour of suit at the V-neck and on the jabot. Black, Independence blue, dark brown. Sizes, 14 to 20, $39.50*

59F42 Delightful afternoon dress of transparent velvet. Youthful hipband slightly shirred at front in basque effect. The flaring skirt, longer at the back and sides, is skilfully achieved by circular godets set in with deep V-points at the hips. A perky bow-knot is perched at the back of the neck. Black, brown, light navy. 14 to 20, $29.50

59F43 *One-piece frock of canton crepe distinguished by a tailored silhouette. Lace at V of neck. Skirt and blouse are fashioned on curving lines with large box-plaits in front of skirt and flare at side and in back. Circular double turn-back cuffs have tiny plaiting repeating the treatment on the surplice collar. Belt consists of two narrow bands of self fabric with metal buckles. Navy, Burgoyne red, Maracaibo brown. Sizes, 14 to 20, $25.00*

70F40 $25.00

59F41 $39.50

59F42 $29.50

59F43 $25.00

59F44 $29.50

59F45 $25.00

59F46 $29.50

59F44 Two-piece canton crepe tunic frock has an all-around plaited skirt. Shirrings and self-covered buttons form an adjustable hipline. Rippling self jabot below the V-neck has a novelty pin. Pin-tucked trimming on cuffs and bottom of tunic is in attractive leaf motif. Black, purple, marine blue. Sizes, 14 to 20, $29.50

59F45 *An ingenious diagonal line across the bodice and skirt gives great distinction to this one-piece canton crepe frock. Graceful circular flounce at bottom of skirt. Shirrings and adjustable tie provide for snug hips. Flattering collar of ecru embroidered batiste with lace edging. Self-covered buttons trim long sleeves. Black, marine blue, rust brown, beet red. Sizes, 14 to 20, $25.00*

59F46 Charmingly youthful one-piece frock of flat canton crepe. The surplice collar is edged with a flared band of matching transparent velvet which terminates in a velvet bow at the hipline. Diagonal strips form a deep, trim hipband. The skirt is knife-plaited all around. Independence blue, brown, black, mountain green. Sizes, 14 to 20, $29.50

A Guide to the Side Lines of Chic

70F33 Two-piece faille canton crepe frock decidedly youthful in silhouette. The becoming roll collar of lighter shade ends in a long tie. The diagonal line of the blouse is attractively fastened with buttons and hand-bound buttonholes. Interesting pocket detail adds character. Skirt is plaited all around. Maracaibo brown with beige, navy with powder blue, or black with white. Sizes, 34 to 44, $25.00

70F34 *The favoured coat dress of flat crepe. Knife plaiting forms a graceful surplice closing and swirls down one side of the skirt and around the bottom of the dress. A very chic line is given by the semi-high waist. Contrasting colour is used for the surplice facing. Black with white, petunia with orchid, brown with beige. Sizes, 36 to 46, $29.50*

70F35 One-piece flat canton dress. V-neck and cuffs are edged in contrasting georgette. Flattering jabot tie of self fabric adorns front of blouse. Wide belt is softly crushed at the side above an effective circular drape. The cuffs repeat the jabot motif. Skirt is novelty group plaited all around. Black with white, navy or mountain green with beige. Sizes, 34 to 44, $25.00

70F36 *One-piece dress of canton crepe for the woman with the fuller figure. Contrasting georgette facing in the V-neck is used with self-fabric to make a double jabot. Two rows of tucking distinguish the shaped hipband which fastens at the side with tabs that have bound buttonholes and novelty buttons. An inserted circular section at one side adds chic to the finely plaited wrap-around skirt. Black, navy, mountain green. Sizes, 38½ to 48½, $29.50*

70F33
$25.00

70F35
$25.00

70F34
$29.50

70F36
$29.50

70F37 Slenderizing one-piece frock of canton. Rippling side drape, cut in one with blouse, is repeated over a contrasting colour. Tucks at each side subtly suggest the waistline and the adjustable tie at the side may be fastened according to individual preference. Irregular circular flounces on the skirt overlap and flare with great chic on one side. The sleeves with circular skirt above the wrist are very new and different. Henna or seal brown with beige, navy with nude. Sizes 36 to 46, $25.00

70F38 *Jacquard crepe frock fashioned on trimly tailored lines. Georgette faces the V-neck and forms a plaited jabot in tri-colour combination harmonizing with colour of frock. Bands of self-fabric are cleverly inserted at center front, back and sides. Inverted plaits in skirt allow freedom. Interesting band motif at cuffs. Brown, mountain green or navy. Sizes, 34 to 44, $25.00*

70F39 A fine quality rep, one of the important light-weight woolen fabrics, is used for this distinctively tailored coat frock. White bengaline fashions the crossed vestee. Interesting detail is manifest in the tucked flare and wrap-around skirt and in the diagonal hipband set on in points to match the sleeve bands. Black or navy. Sizes, 36 to 46, $29.50

70F39
$29.50

70F38
$25.00

70F37
$25.00

67F25
$75.00

70F30
$49.50

63F45
$75.00

59F40
$49.50

70F31
$39.50

SOPHISTICATION SHIMMERS
FROM SHOULDER TO FLOOR

67F25 Evening wrap of metal brocade, much favoured for fall. Furred with flattering shawl collar and cuffs of white hare. Lined with flesh crepe and warmly interlined. Black and gold or green and gold. May be specially ordered in white and gold with beige hare. Sizes, 36 to 46, $75.00. 67F25A Same wrap as above, in black chiffon velvet with white hare. May be specially ordered in American beauty, jade green or Napolean blue chiffon velvet with white hare. Sizes, 36 to 46, $75.00

70F30 *Evening dress in black panne velvet, exceedingly chic this season. Surplice front with low curved back decolletage. The wrap-around skirt is bound by a circular tier draped to the side with shirring to emphasize the normal waistline. Attractive rhinestone buckle and flowers of self-material are effective details. May be specially ordered in aqua green, Lucerne blue or honeydew. Sizes, 34 to 44, $49.50*

63F45 Copy of imported evening wrap in metal brocade with new tight-band cuff and long back. Large pouch collar of hare. White and gold metal or green and gold metal with beige hare. Flesh crepe lined and interlined. Sizes, 14 to 20, $75.00. 63F45A Same wrap in American beauty or Chinese blue chiffon velvet with white hare. Sizes, 14 to 20, $75.00

59F40 *Panne velvet evening dress fashioned with charming femininity. The long bodice is vastly becoming. Shirrings at each hip give softness and fulness. U-decolletage finished in back with a spray of self flowers. A square of the fabric applied in an uneven line at the hip gives a circular effect. Black or chamois beige. May be specially ordered in fandango red or Alice blue. Sizes, 14 to 20, $49.50*

70F31 Evening frock of satin which is destined to have a smart future this autumn and winter. V-decolletage in front, and in low back. Wide tucked hipband fastens in center front with rhinestone buckle. The unusual circular skirt is cut extremely long in back. Flowers of self-fabric and chiffon adorn the hipband at side back. Eggshell, light blue or black. Sizes, 34 to 44, $39.50

67F57
$125.00

67F58
$59.50

67F59
$75.00

67F60
$25.00

67F61
$59.50

Distinctive
Coats of
Dull-Surfaced
Woolens—
with
Furs That
Frame the Face
Attractively
or Drape the
Shoulder

67F57   Richly furred kashmir cloth coat with luxurious shawl collar and deep cuffs. Slender silhouette smartly detailed at the sides. Winter oak brown with beaver or black with Persian lamb. May be specially ordered in black with beaver. Satin lined and warmly interlined. Sizes, 36 to 46, $125.00

67F58   *That the all-black coat is an exceedingly chic choice for fall is readily apparent in this coat of kashmir cloth with its Paquin shawl collar and deep cuffs of black karakul. The modified side-front flare adds decided grace. Lined with black satin and warmly interlined. Sizes, 36 to 46, $59.50*

67F59   A flattering shawl collar and cuffs of kit fox emphasize the youthful straight lines of this kashmir cloth coat. In marine blue or black. Lined with grey satin and warmly interlined. Sizes, 36 to 46, $75.00

67F60   *A classically tailored coat for practical and sports wear is fashioned of a smart tweed mixture. Skilfully designed stitching on collar, cuffs and pockets adds character. Light brown or grey mixtures. Lined with matching satin and warmly interlined. Sizes, 36 to 46, $25.00*

67F61   Soft grey tweed furred with kit fox collar and cuffs makes an ideal town and country coat. May also be had in light brown tweed furred with beaver collar and cuffs. Matching crepe lining. Sizes, 36 to 46, $59.50

Six Fashionable Coats

63F26   The very smart all-black coat of Ramona cloth with slight side-front flare has a semi-shawl collar and cuffs of black karakul.   Black satin lined and interlined.   Sizes, 14 to 20, $59.50

63F27   *Black Norma cloth coat, skilfully tucked and flared at sides. Black fox shawl collar and cuffs. Black crepe satin lined and interlined. Sizes, 14 to 20, $95.00*

Fur Collars May Stand Up Smartly or Fall Back Becomingly about the Shoulders

63F28   Youthful coat of Kashmirelda cloth, flared with great chic at front. Large shawl collar and cuffs of grey krimmer. Black or marine blue with self-colour crepe lining and warmly interlined. Sizes, 14 to 20, $110.00

63F29   *Town and travel coat of a soft nubby tweed. Pouch collar of fur. Large, capacious pockets. Blue and grey with grey wolf collar and grey satin lining, or rust mixture with raccoon collar and tan lining. Warmly interlined. Sizes, 14 to 20, $45.00*

63F30   Slim, straightline coat of Kashmirelda cloth, cleverly detailed at sides. Rich shawl collar and cuffs of fur. Caribou brown with beaver or black with Persian lamb. Self-colour crepe lining and interlined. Sizes, 14 to 20, $125.00

63F31   *Broadcloth coat, effectively flared at side and beautifully framed with shawl collar and cuffs of wolf. Slot seam in back. Brown with eclipse (tan) wolf, black with eclipse (tan) wolf or navy with grey wolf. Crepe satin lined, interlined. Sizes, 14 to 20, $95.00*

Intricate Cutting Achieves the Fashionable Low Fulness

63F26
$59.50

63F27
$95.00

63F28
$110.00

63F29
$45.00

63F30
$125.00

63F31
$95.00

Much Is Made of Intricate Dressmaking Details

70F43 A charming frock of transparent velvet and matching georgette for formal afternoons or informal evenings. The circular skirt of velvet ripples gracefully from a snug hipband over which a girdle is tied at the side. The georgette blouse is effectively appliqued with the velvet. Pert velvet bow at shoulder. Bodice lining of flesh georgette. Black, Independence blue. 34 to 44, $49.50

70F44 *Matching transparent velvet trims the surplice blouse and forms the bow of this gracious one-piece canton crepe frock, which is distinguished by the skilful use of novelty tucking. The circular skirt ends with a circular plaited side drape that gives a smart irregular hemline. A small cream lace vestee adds another note of charm. Rhinestone buckle at side closing. In marine blue, thrush brown or black. Sizes, 36 to 46, $29.50*

67F55 A tweed mixture is chosen for this excellent sports and utility coat collared with fur. Slash pockets. May be worn with or without the belt. Grey mixture with kit fox or brown with beaver. Lined with matching satin and warmly interlined. Sizes, 36 to 46, $45.00

63F37 *Skilful side seaming accents the slim silhouette of this trim, straightline coat of Norma cloth with its huge flattering collar and cuffs of kit fox. Ideal for town wear. Lined with matching crepe satin and warmly interlined. Black or Ensign blue with grey kit fox. Winter oak brown with cocoa kit fox. Sizes, 14 to 20, $75.00*

67F56 An exceedingly smart tweed coat is trimmed with mushroom collar of ringtail opossum fur, youthful belt, stitched pockets and novelty cloth cuffs. Slenderizing seaming features the back. Tan or grey mixture with matching satin lining and warmly interlined. Sizes, 36 to 46, $29.50

67F55 $45.00

63F37 $75.00

70F43 $49.50

63F35 $75.00

63F36 $59.50

67F56 $29.50

70F44 $29.50

63F35 *The new inclination of the mode towards elegance is illustrated in this kashmir cloth coat with its luxurious shawl collar of wolf, its slightly fitted silhouette that flares at the side and its side treatment of fur. Satin lined and warmly interlined. Black with platinum wolf, black with eclipse wolf, starling tan with brown wolf. Sizes, 14 to 20, $75.00*

63F36 Slender straightline coat of Norma cloth, richly furred with a deep shawl collar of kit fox. Cuffs are unique in design and are fastened with button. Tan with cocoa kit fox, black with grey kit fox, Ensign blue with grey kit fox. Matching satin lined and warmly interlined. 14 to 20, $59.50

Coats Are Cut as Elaborately as the Dresses Beneath

70F41 The gleaming surface of satin back crepe is used for the circularly flared wrap-around skirt of this very chic one-piece frock. The crepe side is used for the blouse which is accented by pointed yoke treatment of the satin at front and back. Wide reversible belt which ties at side may be worn with crepe side out for long waistline or with satin side out to achieve new high waistline. V-neck is faced with tucked beige georgette and ends in double-faced tabs. Black or Robin Hood green. Sizes, 34 to 44, $25.00

63F33 *An all-around utility coat of tweed is youthfully belted and has a trimly tailored Johnny collar. The pockets are a smart detail. Matching crepe lined and warmly interlined. Light brown or grey mixtures. Sizes, 14 to 20, $25.00*

63F34 An ideal traveling coat and also exceedingly practical for town and country wear is this brown tweed coat with its distinctive seaming and vicuna fox collar. Tan satin lined and warmly interlined. Sizes, 14 to 20, $29.50

67F52
$95.00

67F53
$59.50

67F54
$75.00

70F41
$25.00

63F33
$25.00

63F34
$29.50

70F42
$29.50

67F52 *A slight front flare makes this black kashmir coat outstandingly smart for fall. To complete the chic all-black note, luxurious black fox shawl collar and cuffs are used for trimming. Finely tailored. Black satin lined and warmly interlined. Sizes, 36 to 46, $95.00*

67F53 The straightline coat that can be wrapped to suit one's individual preferences remains an exceedingly popular fashion. This coat of kashmir is effectively furred with skunk collar and cuffs. Unique tucking down center back. Matching satin lined and warmly interlined. Black or winter oak brown. May be specially ordered in green. Sizes, 36 to 46, $59.50

67F54 *Skilful seaming at the side distinguishes a coat of kashmir cloth trimmed with beaver pouch collar and deep cuffs. Excellent for formal town wear. Light brown or marine blue. Matching satin lined and warmly interlined. Sizes, 36 to 46, $75.00*

70F42 The transparent velvet frock is destined to be a fashionable favourite during the coming fall and winter. This one has a side V-neckline charmingly shirred into a tab and repeated above the double-side drape which gives the smart irregular hemline. Attractive rhinestone pins at neck and side. Black, Independence blue, brown. Sizes, 34 to 44, $29.50